Rave Reviews for
Rage Against the Meshugenah

"Danny Evans has written a moving, funny, and relentlessly honest account of depression. His family must be *kvelling*."
—A. J. Jacobs, *New York Times* bestselling author of
The Year of Living Biblically and *The Know-It-All*

"Danny Evans wrote the book that needed to be written. In *Rage Against the Meshugenah*, Evans goes where most male memoirs don't, recounting the one-two punch of unemployment and depression with hard-won self-awareness. Even in the darkest days of his life, Evans's sense of humor shines through, and his story, while heartbreaking in parts, is ultimately uplifting and hopeful. In short? *Rage* is raw, wry, and riveting."
—Jen Lancaster, *New York Times* bestselling author of
Bitter Is the New Black and *Bright Lights, Big Ass*

"*Rage Against the Meshugenah* is quite possibly a cure for depression all by itself. Danny Evans skillfully tackles the often-overlooked topic of male depression by sharing his own harrowing—but also hilarious—road toward treatment and recovery. A razor-sharp, witty new voice with loads of heart."
—Josh Kilmer-Purcell, *New York Times* bestselling author
of *I Am Not Myself These Days* and
Candy Everybody Wants

"Before reading this book, I thought depression was like other mental illnesses—it only touched a select few of us. Danny's story has shown me that depression is different. It's like an evil genie, lurking inside all of us, waiting to rise

up and take over when we are least able to defend ourselves. Read this book, and I guarantee you that you'll see yourself in his story, because it could happen to any of us, especially in today's uncertain world. Highly recommended."

—John Elder Robison, *New York Times* bestselling author of *Look Me in the Eye*

"Danny Evans demonstrates unequivocally that funny people get depressed, and depressed people don't lose their sense of humor. His memoir is honest and unblinking in its portrayal of how depression colors a life, and yet it is as funny a book as you're likely to read. Wholly original, and a real pleasure to read."

—Robert Rummel-Hudson, author of *Schuyler's Monster*

"*Rage Against the Meshugenah* is a candid, gripping, and hilariously detailed account of what happens when a once-stable family man temporarily loses his mind. A must read for anyone who has struggled with depression, loved someone who has, or just plain loves a great story."

—Amy Sohn, author of *Run Catch Kiss* and *Prospect Park West*

"Way more palatable than Prozac, Danny's true tale of battling depression actually made me laugh out loud on every page. *Rage Against the Meshugenah* was so gripping, brazenly honest, absolutely hilarious, and ultimately hopeful that I ended up read it in one sitting. Who would have thought a book on depression could be downright fun to read?"

—Stefanie Wilder-Taylor, author of *It's Not Me, It's You* and *Naptime Is the New Happy Hour*

"Danny Evans has managed to write a book about depression that is not depressing. Far from it, *Rage Against the Meshugenah* is funny, naughty, heartbreaking and gives the reader a first-class ticket on the crazy train. Better than a double dose of Prozac with a tequila chaser, this book is for everyone who has ever wondered what it's like to fall on your face, stay there awhile, and then learn to stand up again."

—Robert Wilder, author of *Daddy Needs a Drink* and
Tales from the Teachers' Lounge

"Danny Evans is the rare breed of writer who can exhibit both razor-sharp wit and a heart of gold, often in the same sentence. His ability to mix perfectly worded hilarity with sincere emotion and then toss in a few fine-tuned neuroses makes me suspect that he is, indeed, the love child of Dave Barry and Woody Allen."

—Martha Kimes, author of
Ivy Briefs: True Tales of a Neurotic Law Student

"Brutally honest, profoundly insightful, and absurdly hilarious, Danny Evans's memoir of depression is surprisingly not the slightest bit . . . depressing. Evans insightfully writes about his struggle with depression and its side effects with a sort of David Sedarisesque self-deprecating hilarity. *Rage Against the Meshugenah* will be a must read for every man dealing with depression and its side effects, an originally voiced memoir of self-recognition and family love, charming, cocky, and painfully honest, a sort of self-help book on crack, for the modern man."

—Rebecca Woolf, author of *Rockabye*

" 'It takes balls to go nuts,' says Danny Evans. Well, it takes balls to write like this too. With heart, hilarity, and unsparing candor, Danny Evans has managed to plumb the murky depths of modern depression, yet never loses sight of the light (and the jokes) at the end of the tunnel. A great read."

—Rachel Shukert, author of *Have You No Shame?*

WHY IT TAKES BALLS TO GO NUTS

RAGE

AGAINST THE
MESHUGENAH

xx A MEMOIR xx

DANNY
EVANS

 NEW AMERICAN LIBRARY

New American Library
Published by New American Library, a division of
Penguin Group (USA) Inc., 375 Hudson Street,
New York, New York 10014, USA
Penguin Group (Canada), 90 Eglinton Avenue East, Suite 700, Toronto,
Ontario M4P 2Y3, Canada (a division of Pearson Penguin Canada Inc.)
Penguin Books Ltd., 80 Strand, London WC2R 0RL, England
Penguin Ireland, 25 St. Stephen's Green, Dublin 2,
Ireland (a division of Penguin Books Ltd.)
Penguin Group (Australia), 250 Camberwell Road, Camberwell, Victoria 3124,
Australia (a division of Pearson Australia Group Pty. Ltd.)
Penguin Books India Pvt. Ltd., 11 Community Centre, Panchsheel Park,
New Delhi – 110 017, India
Penguin Group (NZ), 67 Apollo Drive, Rosedale, North Shore 0632,
New Zealand (a division of Pearson New Zealand Ltd.)
Penguin Books (South Africa) (Pty.) Ltd., 24 Sturdee Avenue,
Rosebank, Johannesburg 2196, South Africa

Penguin Books Ltd., Registered Offices:
80 Strand, London WC2R 0RL, England

First published by New American Library,
a division of Penguin Group (USA) Inc.

First Printing, August 2009
10 9 8 7 6 5 4 3 2 1

 REGISTERED TRADEMARK—MARCA REGISTRADA

LIBRARY OF CONGRESS CATALOGING-IN-PUBLICATION DATA:

Evans, Danny
   Rage against the meshugenah: why it takes balls to go nuts: a memoir/by Danny Evans.
      p. cm.
   ISBN 978-0-451-22711-9
   1. Evans, Danny—Mental health.   2. Depressed persons—United States—Biography.   I.
Title.
   RC537.E93 2009
   616.85'270092—dc22   2009006118
   [B]

Set in ITC Bookman Std
Designed by Ginger Legato

Printed in the United States of America

For Sharon, Noah, and Julia

AUTHOR'S STATEMENT

This work is a memoir. It reflects the author's present recollection of his experiences over a period of years. To protect the privacy of others (and the ass of the author), certain names, locations, and identifying characteristics have been changed, and certain individuals are composites. Dialogue and events have been recreated from memory, and, in some cases, have been compressed to convey the substance of what was said or what occurred.

MESHUGENAH (meh-*shuh*-geh-nuh) *adjective*

1 mad; crazy: *Jeanette went* **meshugenah** *last night and started peeling bananas with her feet.*

2 mentally deranged; demented; insane: *The neighbors' Chihuahua barked at the wind all night long again. That little yapper is driving me* **meshugenah***!*

[origin: 1892, from Heb. *meshugga*, part. of *shagag*, "to go astray, wander." The adj. has forms *meshugener*, *meshugenah* before a noun.]

PROLOGUE

My first therapist's name was **Neil Diamond,** but he didn't wear sequins, didn't bring me flowers, and most certainly did *not* turn on my heartlight (or any other part of my body). Were he *that* Neil, the *real* Neil, the Jewish Elvis, it would have been my solemn duty as a Jew to dry-hump his leg because that's the kind of *shpilkes* that washes over Members of the Tribe when we are in the presence of Neil Diamond. We go completely *meshugenah*. In fact, there's an obscure, secret Jew code that mandates if you're on a sinking ship in the middle of shark-infested waters with your spouse, your child, and Neil Diamond, and you can only save one of your shipmates, you must save Neil. You can get a new wife and have new kids, but there's only one Neil Diamond. Well, two, actually: the real Neil and the therapist Neil, but the latter, if I'm being completely honest, was kind of a tool. You'd have to get me good and drunk before I'd ever consider dry-humping the leg (or any other part of the body) of a dude who wore deplorable imitation Cosby sweaters and spent most of his time staring at the damn legal pad upon which he jotted notes about his perceptions of my mental acuity. Or lack thereof.

"Are you feeling uncomfortable about attending therapy?" Neil Diamond asked.

"I am," I said.

I was banished to visit Dr. Diamond during high school by my parents, against whom I was mired in an epic battle of wills. More specifically, I was pissed off at them because I thought they were directing my life and education toward a career as a rabbi, which appealed to me about as much as Bea Arthur. Or *borscht* (cold beet soup). Or Bea Arthur cavorting in a bathtub filled with *borscht*, wearing nothing but Estelle Getty's handbag and that saucy Maude scowl. I defied my parents to show me one other "normal" kid in Simi Valley, California, who still went to Hebrew school three nights a week at the age of eighteen instead of engaging in more secular and age-appropriate rites of passage, like smoking pot through a crushed Mountain Dew can and leaving flaming paper bags filled with dog shit on the front porch of the creepy woodshop teacher with the lazy eye and the missing right thumb. I wanted to live a mainstream, borderline immoral life like every other high school kid. I wanted to make my own social choices, my own faith-specific determinations, and my own honest mistakes. Most of all, I wanted to break loose from the vexing, ignominious milieu of Temple Jewey Jew-Jew Hebrew school, where they'd sell you a stale poppy seed bagel for twenty-five cents between classes, but only if you asked for it *in Hebrew*! It's a virtual impossibility to maintain even a faint wisp of street cred when people you're trying to impress hear you say *"ah-nee ro-tzeh bay-gel"* to the blue-haired sisterhood yenta with the Tom Selleck mustache and gefilte fish breath.

"Do I *have* to go to Hebrew school today?" I'd whine to my mother. I tried to look pathetic, convinced it would inspire my mom to believe that giving me permission to skip class would be a saintly, merciful act on par with pardoning a condemned man.

"That's not my decision," she'd say. "Why don't you go ask God? Ask Him if He minds if you just decline to show up at His house this afternoon because you've got more important things to do—like playing that ridiculous Chung King music and looking at those filthy magazines under your mattress. G'head. Ask Him."

(My mother was quite deft at deflecting my attempts at coercion and subversion. When I would tattle on my older sister, Debbie, because she was trying to burn me with her curling iron or because she was blaring her Joni Mitchell cassette tapes so loudly that the drywall between my room and hers was disintegrating, my mom would show me the outstretched palm of her hand and say, "You're driving me *meshugenah* with this! Go talk to the mirror.")

"It's Wang Chung, Mom, not Chung King. Get a clue."

"Oh, I *have* a clue, mister! I *have* a clue. And I'll bet your *father* will have one, too, when he gets home from work."

That was the way things worked in our house: my mom would attempt to reason with Debbie and me, and if she failed (which she often did), my dad and his towering six-feet-four frame would come home and intimidate us into compliance. When even *that* stopped working, they sent me to therapy—which is why I never really gave Neil Diamond a chance. I knew he was solicited as an adjunct to the strong-armed, "resistance is futile" dictatorship that had directed my entire youth. My dad was in complete control of who I was, where I was going, and how I got there. Since my earliest memories, I knew precisely what my future held: I would be a rabbi. I would be a learned Torah scholar who would heed the word of God and tell others why they should do the same. I would marry a Jewish woman (presumably one with a hairy mole on her face), have lots of Jewish babies (please, God, let the mole skip a generation), and make a home (where dairy products and meat reside far, far apart from one another) right next door to my parents' house. This was my destiny. Furthermore, the road to my rabbinical career was utterly devoid of detours. If I was going to be the figurehead of the Jewish community, there was studying to do and prayers to learn and a relationship with God to build and nurture. (Incidentally, I was taught as a boy that God's name is so holy that the simple act of writing the word "God" was somehow sacrilegious and disrespectful. Therefore Jewish prayer books frequently reference the Big Fella as "G-d." Or as I call him, "Gee-Dash-Dee.") The intensity of my studies was to be so sharply focused that it left no time for the frivolous pursuits of a less purposeful boyhood, like playing ding-dong-ditch and toilet papering people's houses and dropping firecrackers down the manhole covers in the middle of our street.

"I don't understand what's so interesting about a bunch of thyroid cases running up and down the floor," my dad said in response to my pleas to watch the Lakers on TV instead of the slumber-inducing, Leonard Nimoy–narrated *In Search of . . .* "Besides, your Bar Mitzvah is coming up and we haven't even finished learning your *haftorah* yet." (It should be noted here with all due respect that those so-called thyroid cases haul in more dough during one forty-eight-minute basketball game than the combined lifetime income of every loinclothed, desert-dwelling, sea-parting goober mentioned in the Torah *and* the whale that swallowed Jonah.)

"How are things at home?" Dr. Diamond asked at the beginning of each session.

"Fine, I guess."

"Mm-hmm, mm-hmm, I see," he said, nodding in faux understanding like a doofus. "And when you say 'fine,' what exactly does that *look* like? Paint me a word picture."

"How do I do that?"

He closed his eyes, sat back in his chair, and took in a deep breath. I assumed this was the behavior he expected me to mimic. "Just close your eyes and tell me what you see," he said.

I don't remember how I responded (perhaps with, "I see a whack job with an overabundance of nose hair and the kind of sweater that gets people killed in other parts of the world"), but I remember thinking this man—the artificial Neil—was a fool. Many years and a few therapists later, I learned that there is an element of performance in therapy. While some shrinks are authentic and down-to-earth, others feel compelled to portray the postures they deem appropriate for each specific patient and his "issue." Some are sensitive and mothering, some are mildly confrontational and challenging, some like to mirror the perceived indecisiveness of the patient. Neil Diamond was just . . . confused. I never got the feeling that he really understood the existential core of my struggle, and my interest in engaging with him therefore dissipated rather quickly. When he would stop to drink some water or make a note on his legal pad ("Patient says Rorschach blot number eight reminds him of a frog who dreamed of being a king, and then became one. Odd."), I passed the time by devising ways to work lyrics from songs by Neil Diamond (the real Neil, not the therapist) into our "therapeutic" dialogue. I never summoned the balls to actually say it, but I fantasized about shaking his hand after our session and saying, "Thanks, Doc. Good times *never* seemed so good."

I drove myself to my therapy appointments in the car I bought with my Bar Mitzvah money—a used Toyota Celica that my sister dubbed "the Chicken Nugget" because of its color, which was a blend of tan, brown, orange, gold, and vomit. It was a color that does not appear in nature. Befitting the car's age and utter lack of coolness, its only built-in entertainment options were a spotty AM radio and an eight-track tape player. I had four tapes, all of which were thrown in as a bonus when I bought the car: John Denver, the Carpenters, Helen Reddy, and the sound track to *The Jazz Singer*, starring Neil Diamond. Serendipitous, no? If I couldn't find the Dodgers game or Lakers game on the radio on the way to therapy, I popped in *The Jazz Singer* and listened to "America," and one time the song stayed with me all the way into the Unreal Neil's* office. I zoned out pretty early on in the session and spent the time pretending I was in the crowd at that big concert at the end of *The Jazz Singer*. (Remember?

---

* There is a phenomenal Neil Diamond cover band called Super Diamond. I've seen them three times. The lead singer sounds *exactly* like Neil—so much so that he has earned the nickname "the Surreal Neil."

"On the boats and on the planes . . . TODAY! . . . they're comin' to America . . . [TODAY!] . . .")

Every time my therapist finished a sentence, I shouted "TODAY!" in my mind.

"Last time we met *(TODAY!)*, you were telling me *(TODAY!)* that you've never kissed a girl *(TODAY!)*."

Unfortunately, even the novelty of that game wore off after a half dozen appointments and I grew frustrated that my parents were still intent on treating me like a little kid, like some idiot who would take off his pants and streak into oncoming traffic if his every thought and movement weren't monitored and reconciled against the behaviors of Abraham, Isaac, and Jacob. And Neil. After about six weeks of therapy, I convinced my parents that Neil Diamond wasn't doing me any good. I may have lied a little bit when I told them it was usurping time that would be better spent on my Jewish education. It's also important to note that despite my frustration with Neil, I was not soured on the concept of therapy in general; I was merely tired of painting word pictures about a part of my life that I knew wouldn't change until I was able to wrest some control away from my parents. But my life did change, at least a little bit, when I got my driver's license. I was granted permission to drive the Chicken Nugget to school and back. Suddenly the world opened up. I had choices, and those I made were mine alone. I stopped most days at McDonald's to get a magnificently nonkosher Sausage McMuffin before school. On the way home I usually went into the liquor store on Cochran Street to thumb through the provocatively glossy pages of *Playboy* and *Juggs* and *Oui*. *(Wheeee!)* Basically, I did what I wanted and I pushed my previously steadfast behavioral boundaries as far as I could.

"Guess what," I said one night at the dinner table. "I'm going to dress up as Santa Claus at the Topanga Mall this weekend."

(Given their allegiance to all things Jewish, I believed saying this to my folks was akin to announcing, "I'm a pre-op tranny and I'd like you to call me Delilah from now on.")

"Oh," my mom said. It looked like she was trying to keep herself from laughing. "Well, you have the perfect build for it."

I was six feet tall, about 150 pounds, and as thin as a No. 2 pencil. As the great Lakers announcer Chick Hearn used to say about Michael Cooper (my favorite player), "When he takes a shower, they have to put a cover over the drain so he doesn't fall through." Nevertheless, there I was a few days later in my fat suit, right outside Orange Julius, sitting in a red velvet throne as one sniveling brat after another climbed into my lap, kneed me in the balls, pulled on my beard, and asked me to bring them a pony or a Barbie doll or a new bike for Christmas. I'd never felt less Jewish, and despite the occasional poopie diaper, projectile spit-up, and morbidly obese kid ("Would you like Santa to bring you some Dexatrim this Christmas, Oliver?"), I reveled in my hours as an artificially rotund, ad hoc Christian. Four months later, I was invited back to be the Easter bunny.

Simi Valley sits just over a hill from the San Fernando Valley, which in turn is just over a hill from the sprawling expanse of Los Angeles. I suppose that makes Simi Valley a suburban suburb, and that's certainly the way it felt as a teenager. Although it is now home to the Ronald Reagan Presidential Library and the courthouse that hosted the Rodney King trial (which sparked the L.A. riots in 1992), it had the vibe of a small town when I was growing up. We had one McDonald's up on Tapo Street, in the same strip mall as the Simi 4 Deli, where all of the Jewish families in town would gather on Friday nights to exchange temple gossip, snarf mustard-slathered corned beef sandwiches, and treat themselves to a special Middle Eastern candy called *halavah*, which is made of ground sesame seeds and honey, and has the profoundly unappealing texture of sawdust. I once believed that just about any food substance could be made exponentially more delicious merely by covering it with chocolate, but one bite of chocolate-covered *halavah* eviscerated that theory altogether.

When those silly magazines come out with their annual surveys of "The Safest Cities in America," it's a pretty safe bet that Simi and/or neighboring Thousand Oaks will be among the top five—a ranking that can be attributed as much to the fact that Simi is home to a significant number of Los Angeles police officers as it can to its somewhat remote geographic location—a forty-minute drive from downtown L.A., which is far enough that hardened Angelinos refer to it as "East Bumblefuck." The only reason to agree with those folks is that Simi was, at least in the 1980s, utterly devoid of cultural relevance, as evidenced by the fact that its most significant architectural landmark when I lived there was Bottle Village*: a small, uninhabitable house built entirely of empty glass bottles in various stages of discoloration from the sun. Grandma Prisbrey, the eccentric, white-haired old woman who started building the place in 1965 because she needed a structure to house her collection of seventeen thousand pencils, was something of a local celebrity, although I privately thought she was a nut job whose "creation" wasn't as much "creative" as it was a testament to the efficacy of the moonshine that was in those bottles before she emptied them.

Labeling someone a "nut job" never warranted a second thought at that point in my life. I frivolously threw that term at friends and enemies alike, usually in jest, but sometimes not. A lot of people do that. An old woman who constructs a house out of empty bot-

---

* Bottle Village was severely damaged in the 1994 Northridge earthquake, six years after ninety-two-year-old Grandma Prisbrey moved on to the big bottle in the sky. The epicenter of the quake was only eight miles away.

tles must be nuts, right? I mean, she must have "serious issues." She's "completely lost it." This armchair psychologist phenomenon is clearly semantic; none of us professes to make a clinical diagnosis when we say, "What is that idiot doing? He must be crazy!" But we each have our private definition of craziness, and in the 1980s my definition was extraordinarily loose and unforgiving. I once had a spirited argument with a friend who thought *Stand by Me* was the *Animal House* of my generation (which it sure as shit was *not*), and even after I presented my lock-solid, slam-dunk case that *Fast Times at Ridgemont High* was a far more accurate representation of the spirit of the time, especially because *Stand by Me* was set in the late 1950s, this asshole simply would not relent. I could have agreed to disagree with him, but it was far easier and far more satisfying for me to assume his attachment to this preposterously flawed analysis was an indication that he was 99.44 percent pure crazy.

These days I'm a lot less likely to call people crazy, even if they are, and that's because I have a sense of what the word really means. Many years after Neil Diamond and Grandma Prisbrey and the mustachioed bagel lady, my severely depressed brain and I walked right up to the shoreline of bona fide clinical madness. I dipped a couple of toes in the water to feel it, and I thought very seriously about jumping into the cold, dark, murky depths. That certainly would have been easier than the alternative: exerting the strenuous emotional and spiritual effort to turn my back to the water and trudge back through the thick, hot beach sand littered with the sharp, fragmented shards of my ego, my dignity, and my sense of who I was. I stood on that shoreline for many months, all the while vacillating over which direction I should turn. There were days when I wanted to take that plunge because it was easier, because it would be far less painful and take a lot less effort than walking barefoot through the sand. But each time I felt like giving in, each time I stripped myself down and prepared to dive into the abyss, I chickened out. I couldn't do it. I had no choice but to turn around, gird myself, and go for it.

It was hard to tell whether I was walking *away from* the darkness or *toward* something beyond the beach, but no matter the impetus, trekking across that hot sand was more grueling and exasperating than anything I'd ever done. I wept. I fell. I bled. Turns out it takes balls to go nuts, but it takes even bigger balls to fight back.

ONE

I **taunted them before I blew their heads off.**

"Hey, John?" I shouted into the office across the hall.

"What?"

"I want to introduce you to a friend of mine," I said in my most polished assassin voice, which was equal parts Clint Eastwood, Tony Montana, and Walter Cronkite. "I call him the Proctologist. You wanna know how he got that name?"

"No! Fuck off!"

"I gave it to him because all he does is tear people new assholes."

Then in one swift movement I pulled the Proctologist from my shoulder, aimed, fired, and blasted John into a fine red mist that spackled the wall and floor where he stood.

"Haaaa! Die, motherfucker!"

"Graaaaw!" John wailed, slamming his fists on the desk. "I want a rematch. Right now."

"Nah, man. I can't. I have a two o'clock with Intel. But I'll be happy to blow you away again when I'm done."

I had developed a reputation as a cold-blooded killer since one of the mouth breathers from IT loaded a futuristic, shoot-'em-up-and-piss-on-their-corpse video game onto the agency's network. We spent our lunch hours blowing each other's heads off. I had killed everyone in the building. They knew I was stalking them, probably saw me coming, but I had a gun the size of an Escalade and there was no way they could escape. It was paradise.

The advertising agency was called Outside the Box, a name derived from a common brainteaser that looks like this:

The challenge with this puzzle is to connect all nine dots with four straight lines, but without lifting the pencil from the paper. The solution, upon which the agency based the entirety of its self-promotion, requires that the line go "outside the box," like so:

"Outside the box" thinking was (and in some circles still is) a buzz term for the intellectual firepower claimed by hundreds of dot-com organizations, although a scant few could actually support that claim with the creative muscle or authentic originality the term implies. Outside the Box Advertising positioned itself as the unofficial home of "outside the box" thinking, as though the agency was the true manifestation of the concept itself and the only ad house on the planet capable of assembling a Web site or a corporate brochure that included the words "pioneer" and "innovative" and "vision." We initiated each new business opportunity by presenting the prospect with the dot puzzle. Few could solve it, but most were sufficiently dazzled by the solution to this baffling visual riddle to do business with us—their rationale being if we could communicate "outside the box" thinking in such an "outside the box" way, we'd certainly have no trouble helping them sell microprocessors or chocolate milk or those pink antiseptic discs that reside in the business end of a shopping mall urinal (official industry name: urinal burgers).

I was making slightly less than a six-figure salary at Outside the Box, more than I'd ever been paid by anyone for anything that didn't involve blow or a ball gag. I had my own office, a fancy title, lots of time to assassinate my colleagues, and a very short walk to the vacant office we'd converted into a Ping-Pong stadium. What I loved about working at the agency was the incessant flow of distraction. Between the Fortune

500 clients, the venture-capital-backed dot-com start-ups sprouting like dandelions, and the aforementioned homicidal make-believe, I didn't have time to worry about the feeling that I was lost in my own life. For at least eight hours a day I could forget that I felt like a guest in my own home, that there was a new baby boy at home about whom I was supposed to be beside myself with joy, but wasn't. Noah and I had no bond, no connection, and the emotional capital I should have been spending on building those ties was wasting away in my self-absorbed self-hatred. I was proud to be his father, grateful to have a healthy son, but I often felt during the first year of his life as though Noah was someone else's kid. I held him and smelled him and stared at him intensely. I tried to will myself into feeling something profound and intense, but all I could feel was emptiness and shame. "You're doing something wrong," I told myself. "Who ever said you were cut out to be someone's dad? Fatherhood is the most important job you'll ever have and you're *blowing* it."

I needed to be distracted from my own brutal self-talk because I knew I couldn't allow myself to listen to it. I'm fragile and sensitive, but consciously knowing this about myself does little to shelter me from harm. I therefore adopted denial and distraction to be my best buddies in times of trouble. I needed to stay occupied. I needed to keep my mind and my hands busy with whatever diversion I could root out, and Outside the Box was a fertile breeding ground for such things. It was my sanctuary. My happy place. Within its boundaries I could completely forget about the crippling storm brewing all around me.

There are no differentiable seasons in Southern California, only varying degrees of perfection. As the low-grade sublimity of the Orange County "winter" gave way to the moderately awesome "spring" months of 2001, the bedrock beneath the dot-com economy turned weak and brittle. Ventures that had arrived on the world's radar with fanfare and awe mere months earlier were exposed as hollow shells—no assets, no business plan, and no long-term Wall Street viability. The opulent thank-you gifts, branded tchotchkes, and free-flowing cases of Heineken our clients regularly toted into the office were gone. The television in the break room, which used to show green, upward-pointing arrows next to the abbreviations for publicly traded dot-com shares as they crawled across the screen, began to broadcast stories of twenty-four-year-old dot-com millionaires who'd lost everything in a matter of days. Investors were indignant. Shareholders were ruined.

I chose to ignore the warnings. Even after our clients began to fade away, most of them leaving tens of thousands of dollars in invoices unpaid, I conditioned myself to believe that my job, my employer, my sanctuary would survive. Opening my eyes to any other possibility would have exposed me to the raw frustration and despair I felt at home. The confusion and self-criticism. The loneliness. The façade of joy and happiness I forced myself to stand behind because that's how a new dad is supposed to look. How can such a lucky man be anything but content? What would it say about a man if he couldn't be happy with a precious baby boy, a gorgeous wife, a nice house with a golden retriever in the backyard, and a well-paid advertising gig? He'd have to be crazy.

"I just crop-dusted a three-year-old."

I'm standing in the lobby of our office building, waiting for the World's Slowest Elevator to slither its way down to the ground floor, and I'm sharing the highlight of my lunch hour with Will, one of the VPs at Outside the Box. Our office is on the third floor of this three-story building and it would be a lot faster just to take the stairs, but Will is the kind of guy who can appreciate a tale like this (even though he's Mormon).

"You *what*?" Will asks.

"I crop-dusted him," I repeat. "Don't you know what that means?"

"No. Please enlighten me."

The World's Slowest Elevator arrives at the ground floor with a resounding thud. *Ding!* The doors open and I nod to Will—the universal sign for "You're older and slower than me so why don't you get on first?" He does so. I get on next and push 3.

"Crop-dusting, William, is when you fart as you walk past someone," I say. "You let the gas out like a crop-dusting airplane does over a field of vegetables or whatever, and leave your scent hanging in the air. By the time your victim smells it, you're already ten steps away. Get it?"

"And you did that to a three-year-old?!" Will says incredulously.

"Well, not on purpose," I explain as the elevator doors open on our floor. "I went to lunch at the mall with a book, and when I came to the end of a chapter and the end of my meal, I looked at my watch and noticed that I still had about fifteen minutes to ride the escalator down to the Apple Store and ogle the merchandise like a lunatic. But the minute I stepped onto the escalator, I felt that familiar little rumble that tells me there's a live one in the chamber. Some little gas bubble was about to earn its wings. And when I stepped onto the escalator, that sumbitch was right at the gate and ready to fly."

"Jesus Christ," Will says. We have stopped in the hallway outside our office door. "Why are you telling me this, Danny?"

"So right then, a mother and her three-year-old son stepped onto the escalator. They were three steps behind me, and right away the fatherly instinct in me kicked in. I knew I had to protect the boy, which is to say I needed *not* to unleash my gastrointestinal shock-and-awe campaign right in his face. But the thing was crowning, man! I mean, it was way past the point of no return. But I clenched my cheeks with all of my might, and when I turned to look again I could see that the boy was clearly inside the blast zone. I was trying so hard to squeeze it."

"And then what?"

"And then I farted. It beat me. The goddamned fart beat me. This invisible but potent cloud of ass wafted into the air, and the poor kid rode right through it. I crop-dusted him."

Will shook his head. It looked like he wanted to say something, but again: he's Mormon. So he simply turned and walked through the door to our office.

It was Friday, September 7, 2001.

Moments after Will and I returned, word spread that we suddenly had a human resources consultant. Given that we were such a small company, HR duties were the domain of Chris, the president and founder. He was an inordinately friendly person, a rather shocking departure from the narcissistic assholes and spineless yes-men for whom I'd worked before (and since) Outside the Box. When I wanted to take a week off to be with Noah after he was born, Chris said take two. One morning, the day after I'd dazzled our biggest client on an important project, Chris walked into my office with a grin he wanted desperately to conceal. He reached out his hand to shake mine, and when he pulled his hand away there was a crisp $100 in mine.

"You kicked ass on this one, Danny," he said. "Go take your wife to lunch. And don't come back until tomorrow."

Needless to say, I was quite satisfied with the status quo of the company's human resources staff.

———

The intercom on my fancy black office phone blared its familiar high-pitched, incoming-call beep, and I presumed it was one of two people: John (requesting another kill shot) or Victoria (the controlling, humorless account manager who saw fit to call me at least once a day for spelling and grammar help) (because looking "confidentiality" up in the dictionary would have usurped too much of the time she'd scheduled for intense brownnosing).

"Hi, uh, Daniel?"

"Hi." A beat. "Who's this?"

"This is Marie," she said. "I'm working with Chris today."

"Oh. Hi."

"Hi. Do you have a minute?"

"Sure. What do you need?"

"Actually, do you think you can meet me in the conference room in like three minutes?"

"Uh . . . sure. . . ."

"Okay, great," she said. "See you then." Click.

Odd. I grabbed my notebook and a pen and opened my office door feeling quite strange about my first interaction with Marie. Figured I'd ask around the office to see if anyone knew what she was up to.

I walked down the hall and into the cubicle farm that housed the agency's graphic designers and administrative staff, and I heard sniffles. I saw two women hugging, and another dabbing the corners of her eyes with a tissue, clearly making an effort not to smear her eye shadow. Having worked with women for almost a decade, I knew that when one woman in the office got her period, all of the other women seemed to get theirs shortly thereafter. I chose not to stop and chat with my coworkers, lest one of them mistake my inquiry for something more hostile and bite my arm off with her bare, hormone-drunk teeth.

Until the moment I opened the conference room door and saw what awaited me inside, the concept of losing my job had never entered my mind. I was a director. Directors don't get fired. Only the peons get fired. I was immune. Duh. But when I walked in and saw Chris on one side of the conference table and this new, stuffy-looking suit named Marie across from him, my obliviousness disintegrated in an instant. If there has ever been a scene in a movie depicting some poor schmuck getting laid off, I'm certain it looked exactly like what I saw in that room.

"Hi. Danny?" the woman said as she stood to greet me. "My name is Marie. Would you like to sit down for a moment?"

I looked at Chris. He looked like a man who'd been punched in the stomach—brooding, uncomfortable, resigned. I pulled one of the black pleather high-backed chairs away from the table and sat down. To my right was a small wicker basket filled with little packages of coffee creamer, artificial sweetener packets, and wooden stirrers. I grabbed one of the mini, tongue-depressor-like stirrers and nervously fiddled with it under the table, rolling it over my fingers like I'd learned to do with a pencil during boring college classes.

"Chris has asked me to come in today to share some news with the team," Marie said. "Outside the Box has been acquired by a company based in Vancouver."

I swiveled my head to look at Chris, to gauge from the look on his face whether this revelation was good or bad. He had a poker face on. I couldn't read anything on it, and the blankness of his expression told me everything I needed to know. I was toast.

Marie belched forth a well-rehearsed monologue of canned boilerplate peppered with faux sympathy (the "we're letting you go" speech must be taught in the first hour of Human Resources 101), but I could barely hear her over my quickening pulse.

". . . and I'm sorry to have to tell you that the new owners have decided that this office will go dark, effective immediately."

She reached behind herself, grabbed a short stack of documents, and pushed it toward me. There was an envelope on top: my last paycheck and two weeks' severance pay.

I once rear-ended an old woman in a Dodge Dart on my way home from high school. I looked through her rear windshield and saw that she wasn't moving, and I was certain that I'd killed her. I figured the force of the impact had caused her to bash her head against the steering wheel and die. I left myself at that moment. Everything moved in slow motion, as though my brain was being so taxed by the reality in front of me that its processing speed slowed to a crawl. (For the record, the old woman was fine.) That was the same sensation that washed over me while I was being dismissed from my job. Evicted from my sanctuary. The earth stopped cold.

When I stood to leave the room, Chris backed his chair away from the table, rose, and reached out to shake my hand.

"I'm really sorry, Danny," he said.

"No," I said. "It's cool. I'll be fine."

Later, when I packed my belongings into a brown cardboard Office Depot box, I stole a stapler, some scissors, and about a dozen packages of yellow Post-its.

It was one thirty in the afternoon.

"What are you doing home so early?" my wife, Sharon, asked as she washed a large soup pot in the kitchen sink.

"They let me go," I said.

"Again? Did they give you another C-note, too?"

"They laid me off, Sharon."

Her eyes opened as wide as I'd ever seen them. They probed me for truth.

"Please be joking," she said.

"I'm totally and completely serious. Chris sold the agency to someone in Vancouver and that person decided to shut down the Irvine office today, for good."

Sharon turned off the kitchen faucet without taking her eyes off me. She grabbed the dish towel to wipe her hands and walked over to where I was standing. I didn't cry. We hugged, which seems like such a basic, innocuous thing—and it *is* for most married couples—but I'm more than a foot taller than Sharon. Her nose jabs into my solar plexus when we hug and all I can see is the top of her head. Variations to that default hug are strong indicators of the state of our marriage. When we're hugging over something happy, she stands on a chair so she can squeeze my neck and I can kiss hers. When I'm feeling romantic (or reasonable variations thereof), I walk up behind her and wrap my arms around her shoulders. When we're making up after an argument, Sharon sits on the couch, I get on my knees in front of her, and I dive in to bury my face in her neck. But this time we simply stood on the grimy tile in our kitchen, leaning into each other, paralyzed by the unknown in front of us.

I met Sharon in the early summer of 1993, about two weeks after my college graduation. With a freshly minted journalism degree and nary a clue what to do with it, I accepted an offer to work as an advisor at the Jewish summer camp I'd attended as a kid. Hidden at the base of the Santa Susana Mountains, the Brandeis Collegiate Institute was a separate, academically inclined entity of the camp, intended for college-aged Jews like me. That summer the staff was asked to arrive a few days early so we could get acquainted, and my eyes first saw Sharon the moment she pulled up in her coughing, mustard yellow Subaru.

"Hi," I said, extending my hand, "I'm Danny."

She looked up at me, flashed the biggest, straightest, whitest smile I've ever seen, and said, "Hi. Sharon."

My normal behavior around girls I liked was very much like the style of the comedian Richard Lewis—lots of pacing and sweating, and a general sense that it would be much easier to be shaved from head to toe and doused with rubbing alcohol than to actually have a conversation with a woman. But I felt more relaxed around Sharon. We took lots of walks, sometimes late at night, and once we sat down in the middle of a sparsely traveled road to watch stars shooting across the sky like bullets. If my life could be measured with the same kind of line graph economists use to measure stock performance on Wall Street, there would be a huge spike at the moment I kissed Sharon's soft, sweet lips for the first time. I'd never known what it meant to fall in love, but within three weeks I was absolutely positive that I was going to marry Sharon—which I did, two and a half years later (shortly after her mother told me in only partial jest that it was "time to shit or get off the pot").

After our wedding we lived in a cramped two-room town house in the same type of cookie-cutter complex for which Irvine is world renowned. We walked to the nearby lake, the health food restaurant with the funny name* and great falafel, and played something loosely reminiscent of tennis on our complex's private courts. Sharon made a concerted effort to do conventionally

---

* Rutabagorz

"wifely" things. She cooked romantic dinners. She put little love notes in the sack lunches she sometimes made for me. We worked out together at a gym frequented by the beautiful (artificially in some cases) people of Newport Beach, including a handful of real live porn stars and Dennis Rodman (if you consider that beautiful). At age twenty-seven, I loved someone and was being loved simultaneously for the first time in my life, and I remember looking at my life in those early years with total amazement. I couldn't believe it had turned out so wonderfully. *Me*, married to a hot blonde! We bought a home. We got a golden retriever. I bought my first brand-new car, a Honda. But I couldn't imagine life getting any better than that. Yet there I was just four years later, wondering if it could get any worse.

"They gave me two weeks' severance."

"Two weeks?!"

Perhaps it was the vulnerability of my situation, maybe the shock and bruised ego from what had just gone down, but something about Sharon's tone pierced right through me. It sounded accusatory, as though she thought I could have negotiated for more severance if I wasn't such a pussy.

"Yes! Two weeks. Sorry if that's not good enough for you! I'm not real happy about it, either."

I stormed off to our bedroom and slammed the door shut. The shades were drawn, the room dark and cold. I dove face-first onto the bed and buried my head in my pillow, desperate for some sort of solace, for some quick replacement for the sanctuary that had just been stripped away from me. I found no such thing. Lying still just gave my mind open water in which to swim with the premonitions of the peril that confronted me—that confronted *us*. My salary was respectable but we could hardly claim even a wisp of financial freedom. Had we decided to settle down in Idaho or Kansas, my salary would have set us in a far more comfortable position. But in Southern California it got us nothing but a precarious paycheck-to-paycheck existence and the pervasive belief that we'd never get ahead and never know true independence. We had amassed only a crumb of savings upon which to fall back. In two weeks we'd be broke.

The issue was too intense to consider, too frightening to imagine. I got up and walked into the bathroom, opened the shower door and blasted the water to the hottest setting my body could withstand. As I waited for the water to warm up, I stripped myself bare and looked into the large wood-framed mirror hanging above the sink. I saw myself as I felt at that moment: completely exposed.

Two

Shane Hutchings had me pinned to the damp ground in his front yard.

"Get off of me, fat ass!"

"Why should I?" He looked down at me with a sinister smirk.

"Because I can't breathe! Get off!"

Shane was my best friend, which a lot of our schoolmates thought was pretty bizarre on account of how strikingly different we looked. I was tall, awkward, and very thin, and Shane, who lived four houses down from me, was a chunky, freckle-pocked redhead. We each had encountered our share of evil taunts from the other fourth-graders because of how we looked, and perhaps that shared understanding of how it feels to be an outcast was what made us such fast friends.

Ours was the sort of boyhood exuberance and insepa-rability film directors tried to re-create in *Stand by Me* and *The Sandlot*. We walked to and from Sycamore El-ementary School together every day. We had sleepovers at each other's houses, one of which ended prema-turely when I knocked over and shattered a crystal candy dish during a pretend grenade war (the gre-nades were rolled-up tube socks). In the summers when the ice cream truck rounded the corner onto our street, Shane and I bought Bomb Pops, sat together on the cinder-block wall next to my house, and laughed at each other's ever-darkening blue tongues.

"Say, 'Shane rules' and I'll get off."

"Shane's a dick!"

He ever so briefly unpinned one of my wrists, slapped my cheek, and then reclaimed his grasp. He knew I was too slight to fight back. I tried to thrust my pelvis up in the air and buck him off, but he had me by fifty pounds. He was in complete control.

"Say, 'Shane rules.'"

"No! Get off!" I yelled as loud as I could, hoping that Shane's dad, who was almost always tinkering in the garage with his vintage Corvette, would hear my wails and come to my rescue. Oddly enough, I'm not sure I ever heard Mr. Hutchings utter a single syllable. He stayed in that garage all day, working on a car he al-most never drove, and I always wondered how he could spend so much time on one project without ever fin-ishing it.

"I'm not getting off until you say it, so just say it," Shane said.

"Fine! Shane rules! Now get off, you fat fuck!"

Shane smiled and began to remove his big ass from my belly, but as he dismounted he reached down and punched me in the left cheek—not hard, but hard enough. I cried and ran off toward my house. It wasn't the pain that caused my tears; it was the violation. Why would he do that? We were friends.

I lost touch with Shane when we got to high school. He was a starter on the football team's offensive line, I was on the speech and debate team, and we just fell in with different crowds. Last I heard he had gone off to Iraq to fight in Operation Desert Storm.

The weekend after my layoff, my thoughts returned to Shane and that day on his front lawn. The feeling of personal violation was strikingly similar. My trust had been trampled. My ally became my abuser. A layoff compares quite favorably to taking a closed fist to the cheek of one's career. The shock is the same. The flash flood of emotions—shock, anger, despair, resignation—sweeps under one's feet at the same rate. There's almost no time for the pain because so much else is in play.

In an instant, I was cut off. My income, my routine, my creative outlet, my friends, my distraction from more existential conflicts—all of it abruptly vanished like a coin in the hands of a magician. Total disorientation. I spent the weekend trying to regain a foothold, very much the way we Californians do in the moment following an earthquake. Is it over? Am I okay? Is my family safe? I wasn't yet equipped to definitively answer any of those questions, but running home to my mommy wasn't an option this time. I'd taken a hit, and I decided the only appropriate response was to stand up and fight back.

Tuesday was my second day of unemployment. I opened my eyes early that morning and forced myself to believe that everything would be okay. I decided not to panic, not to think about having to sell the house and move in with my in-laws. I decided to feel motivated. I resolved before I pulled the covers away from my one-pack abs that this would be the day I'd find a job. The day I took the power back.

I was walking out to the living room when the phone rang. Calls at that hour never portend good things, and I remember thinking about that as I walked toward the phone. Who had died? Who was in the hospital?

"Hello?"

"Hey, Danny, it's Joy."

Joy has been one of Sharon's good friends since elementary school. I crowned her with the nickname "Sassy" one day because of the short, hip, sassy haircut she'd gotten, but her real name is a perfectly true reflection of her character, and I guess I could have used a little joy, given what I'd weathered a few days earlier.

"Morning."

"Are you watching the news?" she asked. It seemed more like an instruction than a question. Her voice was firm, grim, joyless.

"No. I just woke up. Noah's watching *Sesame Street*."

"Turn on CNN," she said. "We're being attacked."

She continued to speak but I heard not a word. I apologized to Noah for having to turn Elmo off for a moment and then pushed 3-0 on the remote control. The screen went dark for a split second while the station changed from PBS to CNN, and suddenly there it was. I stood in the middle of the living room, remote dangling from my fingertips, and watched the acrid black smoke pour from the gaping wound on the side of the building. *Is this real? What is this? What's happening?* Amidst the jibber-jabber of the talking heads straining to speak articulately through their own shock, one said something about "taking another look." Her utterance was immediately followed by a taped replay of an airplane flying into a skyscraper.

And then another.

I dropped the remote control.

"Wiss Emmo, Dah-dah?" Noah asked.

"Elmo went bye-bye, buddy. I need to watch this instead."

As the hours of coverage went by and the shock of what happened that morning gave way to haunting reality, I felt myself sliding down. Physically. Emotionally. Spiritually. It was as though I was at the top of a greased pole, trying to hold on to the top, straining to keep myself from slipping all the way to the bottom. For a few days I found solace in the crush I had developed for Ashleigh Banfield, the bespectacled blonde on MSNBC. But that too vanished over time, and I was left with nothing but a dead spirit. Nothing but despair for humanity. Nothing but nothing. For six days I sat on our faded blue denim couch (the first home furnishing Sharon and I ever bought together), retreating only for sleep, food, and the bathroom. My eyes swallowed it all. People jumping. Buildings collapsing. New Yorkers posting flyers with pictures of their husbands, mothers, uncles, each with some variation of the language of despair. *Missing. Please Help. Have You Seen My Sister?* As the days melted into one another and the dust and smoke dissipated, I watched the faces of the same terrorized citizens change. Reality set in. They were gone. The flowers against the fences withered and blackened in perfect time with the sense of hope. The cable news networks loved it. *If it bleeds, it leads.* If we can stick a microphone into the face of a bereaved wife, ask her callously if she had any idea while kissing her husband good-bye as he left for work Tuesday morning that she'd never see him again, and then capture on tape the gravity of the past few days overwhelming her, we'll have a perfect teaser for the ten p.m. town hall meeting with Wolf Blitzer. Brilliant! America will be captivated and the advertisers will be breaking down the doors to get on our air.

I grieved for more than the thousands of extinguished human lives that week, more than the death of the America I grew up with. I grieved the death of decency. I grieved that I was going to have to raise my son in a world where people can commandeer airliners and fly them into hundred-story buildings, and where the grieving of families victimized by such inhumanity is broadcast on live television, brought to me with limited commercial interruption thanks to Wal-Mart, and interpreted by Sanjay Gupta. All of a sudden, *bam!*, the world has no soul, no sympathy.

As the years have passed, I have wondered what I looked like during this horrendous string of days. What did Sharon see when she looked at me then? I have always been a news and sports junkie (I worked as a newspaper reporter during the first full year of my courtship with Sharon), but my attentiveness to the coverage from Manhattan was so far beyond the bounds of simple interest; I was in a trance. I watched with the focus of a snake charmer, intently studying the cobra's eyes and sways for even the slightest inclination to strike. Nothing else existed around me, and my gaze never left the TV screen. I wonder at what point my focus stopped being typical fascination and empathy and metamorphosed into something more desperate. I wonder when I stopped being curious and started being mentally ill. I don't know when it happened, but I have an extraordinarily clear recollection of when it first entered my consciousness. I wasn't the hardened narcissist my post-9/11 attitude reflected, but I now believe this line of thought was the first little sapling of my free fall into depression. The selfishness of the thinking is horrifying to me now, but it was real: I began to look upon losing my job as my own personal 9/11. I drew parallels between them—the suddenness of the attack, the lack of preparedness, the obliviousness to warning signs before the incident, and the resounding disintegration of what once stood mighty and proud. At some point during the hours and hours I sat watching the coverage, I decided I was a victim, too. I had been attacked, and I was missing. *Have You Seen Me?*

THREE

Near the end of *Taxi Driver*—about ten minutes before Robert De Niro solicits Jodie Foster for some underaged lovin' and is directed to take the matter up with her pimp, Harvey Keitel—there's a short scene that looks a lot like how it feels to sink into clinical depression. De Niro's Travis Bickle sits in his slovenly apartment, slouching in his La-Z-Boy and holding a gun in each hand. The television is on (tuned to *American Bandstand*) and Jackson Browne sings "Late for the Sky" in the ether. The scene's realism comes from De Niro's eyes; they're directed at the TV screen in front of him but he's not actually watching it. He's looking *through* it. He wears the hollow, thousand-mile stare of a man crumbling in real time; he is present physically but his mind is elsewhere. He has turned inward, and here is the magic of Scorsese's direction: we are left to imagine what sort of madness is occurring in De Niro's mind. That's how mental illness feels, too. The body is clearly in the room but the mind is . . . not. The body and spirit disconnect, and without each other they atrophy and wilt like an Easter tulip in May.

But depression doesn't happen all at once. It slowly and methodically overpowers the brain, like a boa constrictor tightening its grip on an unsuspecting rodent until the fuzzy, unlucky prey can no longer breathe or muster a fight. To the outside world, a man sliding into depression may look just like De Niro: lost inside himself, deep in thought, zoned out. It does feel that way sometimes, but eventually the depressed mind becomes the helpless rodent. Control is lost and one's very existence is at the whim of the predator.

Gradual though the process of becoming depressed may be, for me there was a watershed moment—a particular instance when it finally became irrefutably clear that my mind had gone rogue. At the first instant of coherence on the morning I hit rock bottom, I felt as though I was covered by a blanket of bricks and cinder blocks, as though gravity had been hacked overnight by some computer nerd with greasy hair and Cheetos hands, and the weight of the entire world and all of the stars and planets and satellites had fallen directly onto my head and body. I could feel that tremendous burden in my bones, in my muscles, in every cell of my being. I blinked my eyes several times to make sure I wasn't having a nightmare. If I was, I hoped that I might wake up from this agony, perhaps to realize that the feeling I'd had was a deep, in-dream metaphor for something I would be able to interpret in my waking moments. Maybe I was too stressed. Maybe this was the universe telling me to treat my wife better or drive more carefully or run away from something dangerous. But the constant, purposeful blinks had no effect. I was awake. This was real.

What is this? What's happening to me? Have I gone crazy?

I eat a diet that would send shudders through even the most hardened, carnivorous sloth. If given the opportunity to start my own religion, I would decree that we gather each week at Taco Bell to give praise to the Whopper and "baptize" new converts to the faith in a pool of Arby's Horsey Sauce. We would believe in the might of the Hamburglar, the healing power of the Slurpee, and the pure evil that lurks in anything involving the use of silverware or vegetables (not counting ketchup). Sadly, my allegiance to this faith means I am often prone to stretches of lethargy and sugar crash. But the energy depletion that overcame me as I awoke that morning was far beyond anything I'd ever known. That Cheetos-handed nerd must have tripped on an electrical cord during the night and unplugged the imaginary cord that connected me to anything in life that gave me energy or optimism or pleasure. My mind felt physically heavy. I had an all-consuming sense of desolation, as though my soul was made of lead, but somehow it also left me feeling empty. Vacant. It was as though I was dying from the inside out and watching every second of it. I was a witness to my own demise. The morning sunlight peered through the edges of the window shade, daring me to come outside and be bathed in its glare, but I stayed on my back and stared at the ceiling. The texture of the drywall. The warps and imperfections. The bucktoothed shadow cast by the ceiling fan. The simple act of turning over required a lengthy pep talk to myself, like a fire-and-brimstone football coach stomping around a locker room, pumping his players up moments before the championship game.

If you can do this, you're still alive. Come on. Do it. Go.

I finally pulled it off, rolling from my back onto my belly, but the exercise left me exhausted and frightened. I buried my face in the pillow for the fifteen minutes that followed.

I had to take a piss. The toilet was exactly seven paces away from the edge of our bed, but when just flipping over was like running a marathon, sitting up and walking seven paces was a hike across the Sahara. The sadness, the weight, the fear, was physically heavy.

I can't handle this. What's happening to me?

Only a few months earlier I was playing full-court basketball for forty minutes straight. I was fit. I was strong. I ran like a spaz and missed every shot I took, but I was mean. Yet there I was that morning, maybe a hundred days later, struggling just to get up and relieve myself.

Is this how crazy feels? Is this what it's like to go mad?

I shook my head from side to side like that dumbass cartoon coyote does when an anvil falls on his head, in hopes of snapping myself out of it.

Come on, you stupid piece of shit! Come on! Please!

Sharon came in to check on me. I heard the door open slowly, its bottom edge running over the shag of our tan carpet. I saw her shadow disturb the ray of sunlight peeking in through the curtains.

"How are you doing?" she asked, placing her open palm on my back.

"Not good," I said into my pillow. "Not good."

"Can you tell me what's going on? What do you feel?"

Open-ended questions like this one had become an irritant to me. My temper was tinder, dry brush, and having to explain myself was an errant cigarette butt flicked out the window of a passing car. I was too exhausted to string together more than five or six words, too confused and frightened to understand this new reality myself, let alone explain it to others.

"I feel nothing," I said. "But I'm starting to think I might need to go to the hospital."

I can't handle this.

When discussing addiction and dependency, those who are trained to help people heal are keen to remind us that an addict can't truly begin to rehabilitate himself until he has hit "rock bottom." I've scoffed at that term my whole life. I always believed it was the type of jargon people throw around when they're not smart enough to fix the problem. I don't think that way anymore. It's not true.

Rock bottom is real.

You don't know what it looks like ahead of time, but you know it when you get there. It's a voice without a sound. It walks out of the shadows, places its warm hands on your cold cheeks, looks you dead in the eye, and says, "You need help."

I stood in front of the bathroom mirror and looked at my face. Again I shook my head violently from side to side, hoping that somehow whatever had shorted out inside would fix itself. When we were kids, my sister introduced me to "the five second rule," which dictates that when you're eating something and a piece of it falls to the ground—a piece of cookie or the chunk of a melting Popsicle that slides off the stick—you can still eat it if you pick it up before five seconds have elapsed. If you catch it in time, you can rescue it before the cooties get all over it. Maybe the same would apply here, I thought. If I could snap whatever was broken back into place before too much time passed, maybe I could salvage myself. But as my moods and outlook retreated further and further into the fog, I could feel that my brain had been on the fritz too long to be retrieved. I couldn't rescue it.

We're told during the peak of every fire season in Southern California that a wildfire creates its own wind. It propels the blaze farther, faster, and gives it the extra gusto it needs to carve a wider swath of destruction. My depression was the emotional parallel of that devilish wind. I was sad about being so god-damned sad, and that sadness duplicated itself so many times over that every fiber of my emotional fabric was occupied by this single sensation. My spirit was so heavy that the emotions one would normally summon to pull oneself out of depression—hope, enthusiasm, pride—had nowhere to go. They atrophied. They shriveled up and died. And that was sad, too.

I was desperate for what had died. For the enthusiasm I needed to help me find a job. For the pride I needed to tell me it was time to shape up, for my kid's sake if not my own. For the hope I needed to keep me from giving up. I was helpless without these spiritual staples. I felt like a man in a straitjacket, and my body followed these emotional defections with its own physical cave-in. I wasn't hungry. I wasn't cordial. My temper was short, and over time the simple act of getting out of bed became too challenging to even consider.

I remembered feeling excited about life. I was proud of myself and what I had accomplished. But in the span of just a few weeks, I was rendered impotent to live with even a wisp of gusto—and I wondered to myself if life was worth living without it.

FOUR

It takes balls to go nuts. I don't believe you can know this at the time you're actually plummeting into mental illness, but you learn shortly after your arrival that depression and its ilk are not for the faint of heart. Though you may be weakened, you have to stay tough enough to tolerate the truth that most people can't understand what the hell is going on with you. The simple act of *talking* about your ailment requires an uncommon amount of bravery, never mind the added frustration that attempting to communicate the way depression feels to the average Joe is like trying to communicate in a language you don't know. If you're going to get depressed, I suggest you put on a cup.

I lost myself inside myself, and any time I was challenged to describe exactly what I was feeling I was utterly lost for words. And because I couldn't explain how I felt, I often heard alternately worded variations on the same infuriating theme: "Snap out of it, Danny. Pull yourself together, Danny. Be a man, Danny." This, for me, is the single most miserable aspect of depression— no one understands it. The people to whom one would normally turn for help in crisis cannot comprehend the depth of one's pain. When the helpers can't help, the darkness deepens. So then what? How could I behave decently when I was broken and alone? How could I choose to behave decently when virtually every critical, cognitive thought processor—logic, concentration, reason, memory, belief—was lying flat on the canvas while its opponent danced around the boxing ring in celebration?

I awoke with a modicum of anticipation each morning, wondering if it was the day when I'd feel like myself again, but it wasn't. It never was. Every day was a carbon copy of the one before it, like Bill Murray in *Groundhog Day*, but without the laughs. I had a repeating fantasy that someone would come around and scoop me up, take me somewhere, put me to sleep with a strong drug and not wake me up until I was better. I saw a movie once where the crew on a spaceship blasted off to a destination in deep, deep space. Since the ride was so long, the crew members were put into a lengthy sleep coma and kept that way for many years. When the spaceship finally reached its location, someone in an earthbound mission control center pushed a button that woke the astronauts up. That's what I wanted.

That's what I craved. But as I learned through therapy, that faraway destination, Planet Happy, couldn't be reached on autopilot. I'd have to be awake for the whole trip—through the turbulence and the darkness and the unbearable fluctuations in cabin pressure.

Though it was clearly broken, my mind involuntarily got up off of the canvas and said, "If this numbness is the only thing I can feel, I'd rather feel nothing at all." My need for relief was more dire, more acute than adherence to the standards of good taste and morality and setting a good example. I needed anesthesia. I needed an addiction to take my mind off of my mind.

Fortunately, I'm too big a wimp to take any drug stronger than marijuana or Tylenol PM. I therefore eliminated heroin, meth, and cocaine the moment they crossed my mind. I would have sniffed glue but I don't like the smell. Perhaps I could have become a workaholic . . . *if I had a job.* Finally, I found something to take away my pain, and I found irony in the fact that after all of the searching and thinking I'd done, the answer was in my pants all along.

To me, pictures of bare breasts were like manna from heaven. Pictures of freshly shorn crotches spread apart between some slut's index and middle fingers were the best painkillers I could get without a prescription or a handgun. *Depression? What depression?* I became a porn junkie, which at its core is no different from any other addiction. I surfed in secret. I spent money to join especially hard-core sites or those dedicated to a specific model or porn star. I told myself I could stop whenever I wanted to, but why would I want to? Porn made me feel better. It gave me back the feeling of machismo that had been stripped from me. It made me forget that I was miserable and hopeless.

Sharon held on to her part-time job, and in the mornings when she went off to work, I plopped Noah down in front of Buzz Lightyear and retreated to my office for my own perverted version of daytime entertainment. *Here, Buzz. Raise my son. To infinity . . . and beyond!* Thanks to the glory of the Internet, I quickly developed a short list of favorite porn stars: the popular blonde with huge tits and the barbed-wire tattoo, the skinny redhead who squirts, the brunette who moans like she's having her appendix removed with a melon baller. These women were my Prozac. When everyone else around me wanted something from me, needed something from me, had some kind of criticism or disdain for my behavior, all my starlets wanted was to please me. That was the kind of relationship I needed. We didn't have to speak or analyze or get me "better"; the only work to be done was fast-forwarding over the talking parts.

Depression? What depression?

I didn't masturbate very much.* For me, porn was more about control than, ahem, ejaculating. I could put myself into any lurid scenario I saw on the Internet. If the starlet was ugly or loud or otherwise unat-

---

* Hi, Mom.

tractive to me, I could find something better. If she was hot, I could envision myself in the scene with her, altogether ignoring the differences between the muscular, well-endowed dude on-screen and my own frail little peashooter. As far as I was concerned, I was Adonis and every slut in Spoogieland wanted to run her Bedazzled acrylic fingernails over my washboard abs (which in reality are just my ribs poking through my skin, but what*ever*).

To feed my porn addiction with other media, I mapped out which liquor stores in town sold magazines and DVDs, and I frequented them, always looking for the next hottie, the next new painkiller, the next buzz.

"How you are doing today, man?" one store manager said. "Back for more of the girls, yes?"

"Yeah," I mumbled as I stared at my shoes. There are two places where men should absolutely not make eye contact or talk to each other: between stalls in a public restroom and in the porn section of the liquor store. In each of these locations, men do things that should neither be discussed nor watched.

The Manager With No Interpersonal Boundaries turned around, opened a drawer, and retrieved a DVD in a plain white sleeve.

"I give you gift because you are loyal customer, man," he said. "You like this one. It will have lots of *ahnool*."

"Lots of what?"

"*Ahnool,*" he said again. "In the eh . . . the eh . . . the bot."

"Oh. Anal!"

"Yes, yes. *Ahnool.* Forgive me. My English not so good."

Other, more mature men may feel differently, but for me the experience of buying porn is like going into a supermarket and buying *only* a tube of root-beer-flavored sex lube or approaching a Barnes & Noble cashier with *only* the August issue of *Jizzbomb* magazine. It can't help but draw attention to you, and I didn't want any such attention. Since I spent so much time in liquor stores and wasn't too keen on developing a reputation as a perv, I made it a practice to take home a twelve-pack, a case, a thirty-pack of beer from time to time. The next new painkiller. The next new problem.

FIVE

I drank Bud Light. Two was the minimum; I needed at least a couple to even consider getting through the night without ending up a huddled mass of tears and snot in the fetal position on the kitchen floor. Three made me a little more relaxed, and four began to make my vision a wee bit fuzzy around the edges. But to really do the job, to truly stun my brain into submission, I needed to finish the six-pack. I began to crave the taste of Bud Light and look forward to five or six o'clock ("beer thirty," as the kids call it) because that was, as everyone knows, the time when someone can reasonably start drinking without looking like they have a problem. Alcoholics drink all day, I surmised, but those in complete control can wait until the sun starts to descend into the Pacific.

It's not a problem. I can stop anytime I want to.

Sharon spiritedly disagreed with me. From her perspective—from the perspective of a mother and a responsible adult and someone who cared about me more than I did at the time—it most certainly *was* a problem. I steamed about the fact that we had lived completely opposite drinking lives until that point. Sharon started drinking in high school, sometimes even sharing a six-pack of beer in the parking lot with her friends before they all wobbled in for badminton team practice. Having started so early, she was no longer terribly enamored with alcohol. She drank socially, but not heavily and not frequently. Conversely, I was squeaky clean during high school. I had no popularity to speak of (unless you consider my tenure as Chief Dork of the speech and debate team popularity) and was therefore never invited to the types of parties where my classmates would be drinking. When I went off to college at Fresno State University, where there's nothing to do but get wasted* and go cow tipping, drinking became part of my life. I was a late bloomer when it came to alcohol.

"Do you want Noah to see you like this?" she asked from the kitchen. The scent of steamed broccoli wafted through the house as she prepared dinner, which I

---

* The liquor store across the street boasted on its outdoor signage that it was the home of the world's largest Coors Light display. That was either pathetic or awesome, depending on your blood-alcohol level.

was ruining for myself by eating Lucky Charms straight from the box.

"Oh, come *on*," I said. "He's one year old. Do you remember anything from when you were one?"

"No, but that doesn't mean what happened then was meaningless. You remember things subconsciously, Danny. It matters."

It's pretty humiliating in retrospect. The need for relief was so raw, the judgment so completely clouded, the pain so close to the surface that I found myself fighting to prove the negative—to make a case *in favor* of excessive drinking. I'd like to believe there isn't an ambulance-chasing defense attorney in the Western hemisphere who would take such a turkey of a case. It's like trying to prove that the earth is flat. But at the time I was making these arguments to Sharon, I genuinely believed what I was saying to her.

"Whatever," I said. "You see it your way, I see it mine."

I couldn't let her be right, even though she was. I was very protective of my drinking, so much so that I developed a line of boilerplate rationalizations to fall back upon when Sharon challenged me (as she often did) on the frequency and quantity of my consumption. I knew her questions. I had asked them of myself. But at the time it was more important for me to have what I needed to numb my pain than it was to engage in serious self-analysis or to repair my moral compass.

"You know alcohol is a depressant, right?" she

asked. I could hear the desperation in her voice. It hurt me to hear her that way.

"What are you worried about?" I said. "I'm here in my own home. I'm not driving anywhere or operating heavy machinery. I'm not going to do anything stupid. I'm fine. Seriously. I'm fine."

"You're *not* fine! You're drinking too much, Danny! This is not okay with me!"

"Sharon, you're Noah's mother, *not* mine. *I* decide what I put into my body and I think I'm perfectly capable of determining when I've had enough. I'm sorry that doesn't comply with your standards, and if it's really *that big* a problem for you, there's the door."

I didn't want to concede the point or give in to her. That somehow became very important to me. All I could see was her trying to take away the only thing about myself that I could control anymore, and that pissed me off royally.

"Lovely," she said. "You're picking beer over me? Are you sure you want to do that?"

"Look, you have *no* idea what I'm going through right now."

"You're right! I have no idea! Because you won't talk to me about it!"

"How can I talk about it when I don't even know what it is myself?" I was yelling. "All I know is that I feel dead and hollow and I've lost control of everything in my life. I can't control my brain, I can't control my son, I can't control our income, my employment situation, my sleep schedule, *you*. . . ."

"Do you think drinking beer is going to help you get that control back? Do you think staring at naked women on your computer all day is going to fix what's broken?"

This singular issue—my porn habit—was extraordinary tinder, but not because Sharon is a prude, sexless woman; she most certainly is not. The volatility was rooted in the very earliest of Sharon's memories. Her father, George, a respected physician and father of four, suffered a heart attack while playing tennis and died suddenly. Sharon was four years old, the youngest of her siblings. Naturally, the devastation of his loss left lasting damage on each member of her family, and on the family as a whole. So tragic was George's passing, so painful was the loss, that the family avoided discussion of the event as a coping mechanism. Perhaps their subconscious minds believed that by ignoring the grief they could make it hurt less. As decades passed, avoidance of sorrow and pain became a family hallmark—and it most certainly resurfaced when Sharon became aware of my lascivious online behavior. Although I continued to tell her how gorgeous and sexy I thought she was, her gut told her that something wasn't quite right—that I was saying such things simply to appease her, not because I meant it. Late one night, after I'd gone to bed, Sharon went to my computer, looked at my browsing history, and found confirmation of what she suspected. As she revealed in therapy much later, that discovery triggered in her feelings of insecurity, disappointment, and anger. But instead of confronting me with these harsh realities, she instinctively reverted to the behavior modeled for her as a child. She stayed quiet. She gave me my space. She said she thought doing so might help me in some way, but in fact it made her feel more isolated and insecure. This, for me, was the most crushing blow to come from our joint therapy sessions. It was one thing to commit crimes against myself; what did I care? But the revelation that I brought real pain to Sharon is my greatest regret from this dark period in my life.

"Oh, come on, Sharon!" I said. "Like I'm the only guy who looks at porn?"

"I'm not worried about what other guys do. I'm worried about *you.*"

This is where I wish I had stopped myself. I wish I would have heard and internalized her last two sentences and realized that if something I was doing caused her concern or embarrassment, it was time to stop. Perhaps the normal Danny, the Danny I was pre-depression, would have responded in a loving, respectful way. But I was not that Danny. Rather, I was the Danny who believed he could rationalize his way out of anything. I thought intellect was kryptonite to hurt feelings. I thought I was smarter than Sharon, so much so that I could even convince her she wasn't seeing what she thought she was.

Her: "You're watching too much porn."

Me: "It's not like I'm sleeping with other women, Sharon. I'm looking at dirty pictures. Big deal. If I get the urge to have sex with someone, you'll be the first to know."

Her: "You're drinking too much."

Me: "Too much for who? It's not as if I'm going out driving or becoming violent or using illegal substances. I'm an adult sitting in my own house and watching television. If that's a crime, it's a victimless crime for sure."

I recall these conversations vividly, and what strikes me most in retrospect is that I truly believed what I was saying to Sharon. Aren't those the tactics of an addict? Was it really *that* bad? The answers are difficult. Although I don't believe my drinking ever reached a level of volume or "need" strong enough to fit the conventional definition of alcoholism, I was certainly dependent upon it. In time I learned how to cope with stress in a more adult way, but early in my depression I seemed to need the comfort of a beer can (or four) the way a baby needs his pacifier. And I ultimately found a way to make myself believe my drinking was harmless.

The convergence of Sharon's position (that I needed to control myself) with mine (that I was in total control) created an uneasy stalemate. Sick or not, I was a grown man. I was going to do what I wanted, and I wanted to drink.

"You need to get some help, Danny." She was pleading. It was no longer a fight; it was an intervention. "Whatever you're doing on your own isn't working for you. Look at you. You're miserable."

SIX

After two full days of cavorting in bed with my new pal Major Depression, my rank body odor became so fierce that I had no choice but to peel myself off of the mattress. I seized the opportunity by going to the store for more beer. The radio came on when I turned the ignition over and I heard the familiar frenetic thumping of "Hot for Teacher," an old Van Halen song that always gets my fingers drumming on the steering wheel (usually out of time with the song, but that's my issue, not yours). When Eddie Van Halen's timeless guitar solo started to wail out of the speakers of my Honda CR-V, I thought about gripping the diagonal part of my seat belt and playing along with him. But my heart wasn't in it. There was no music in me.

As I made the left turn out of the neighborhood and stopped at a red light, I started to cry, right there in the middle of Eddie shredding like a motherfucker. I had no idea why it was happening, but it felt kind of good. And also embarrassing.

The light turned green, but the intersection is notorious for having the fastest green light in recorded history. Only three cars made it through before it turned yellow, and I was stuck there for another cycle. Eddie was starting to bug me, starting to make me feel that I was no longer me, and I wanted not to think about that. To drown him out, I pushed the button that engages the CD player. I knew there had to be something chipper in there, although I wasn't sure what disc I'd put in.

A song came on. There was a man's voice. He was pleading.

It was Adam Duritz of the band Counting Crows. I'd always felt a strange connection to Adam because he seemed to be an emotional guy, and because he was so gifted at expressing his emotions in his lyrics. I empathized with a lot of what he wrote, felt like we were very much alike in a spiritual way. But this song, "Have You Seen Me Lately?," was always a bit of an enigma to me. I was never able to distill it down to a simple explanation about why he felt so lost and desperate, but given where I was and how I'd changed, it made perfect sense this time. He sang about his own pitiful, misguided assumption that someone would have noticed if he'd disappeared. His own recollection of himself was a colorless outline, and that section in particular caught me in a tender spot. *My* world had gone completely gray. *I* was missing. I needed someone to notice, to say something, to "color me in": "Could you tell me things you remember about me? And have you seen me lately?"

I began to cry again. It was not the cry of a normal guy, not a sniffle and a tear diving down my cheek. It was the kind of cry that lets you hear the sound of the sadness in your body and it surprises you, frightens you, changes you. My body was talking to me.

It's time, it said. *It's time.*

SEVEN

"**D**anny, we need to talk."

"What about?"

"I think you know," she said. "I know you're not feeling well and you probably don't want to talk about this right now, but it's been two months, honey. Your severance money is gone and I just had to transfer funds from our savings to cover the mortgage."

I gritted my teeth. Every married couple has its one consistent conflict, and for us it was money. In simplest terms, Sharon is the saver and I am the spender. One of her first acts of heroism in my life was teaching me how to pay off the credit card debt I amassed in college. It was not a terribly ominous sum—around $1,000, I think—but by then it was pretty clear that we were going to spend the rest of our lives together and

Sharon would sooner have married a garlic-scented eunuch than a man with a blemish on his credit report. These many years later, she was still watching my spending like a hawk, but I had established at least a buffer of credibility by claiming the role of sole bread-winner while she raised Noah. Suddenly, that credibility evaporated. Even worse than continuing to spend money, I wasn't winning any bread. We were hemorrhaging through my hands.

"What do you want me to do?" I asked angrily. "I'm scared, too, you know. I'm scared of what's happening in my *head*! Believe me, I know what our accounts look like and I know your tendency to freak out when it gets a little tight, but—"

"*A little tight?* Did you *hear* what I just *said?* We are running out of money, Danny."

I'd like to think that in normal circumstances I would have been resistant to the idea that Sharon should work full-time instead of being home with our baby. Aside from the hit such a scenario would plant right on the glass jaw of my self-respect, it would devastate Sharon. During our courtship and the early years of our marriage, it was understood that our children would be in their mommy's care at least until after kindergarten. It was an easy commitment for me to make because Sharon is spectacular around children and I wanted—I *needed*—our children to be with her in their most formative years. Ripping her away from that and making her go to work would have broken her heart.

I was keeping something from her and I couldn't bring myself to say it. I knew I was hurting us by not finding work. I knew we were in trouble and I would certainly have rallied to the rescue had my emotional state not deteriorated to the point that I couldn't find it in myself to look for a job. The financial peril resulting from my condition further dampened my spirit, too. I began to conjure images of sleeping in our minivan and begging for money on street corners—which simply piled despair and hopelessness on top of my depression. All my life I'd had a healthy fight-or-flight reflex, but it was as if someone had chosen flight on my behalf. My spirit waved the white flag of surrender. I couldn't tell her that. She'd freak, and that would in turn hurt Noah. She was the only stability in our home and there was no way I was going to sabotage that by telling her that looking for a job was as far a leap from reality as I could fathom.

"You know, I've been carrying us financially for quite a while now," I said angrily. "I need help now. I'm having a problem, and maybe instead of telling me how bad I'm screwing up, you could step up and take the breadwinning role for a while."

"Danny, listen. I love you and you know I'd do that in a heartbeat if I could, but who's going to watch Noah all day?"

"*I* will."

"Oh, come *on*, Danny! You're having trouble finding

the strength to get out of bed these days. Caring for a toddler takes a lot of effort and patience and I don't think you have much of either right now."

She was right, obviously, but I chose to be offended. I chose to be macho about it because I wanted to feel something and anger was the only emotion I could summon. Beggars can't be choosers.

"How the hell do *you* know what I have?"

It creates its own wind. Like a wildfire.

Sharon's strength and hard-line posture toward my troubling behavior belied her own fear about what was happening to me. To her. To us. I was almost entirely oblivious to her struggle because I was so focused on my own, but I now know that loving someone who's depressed is like the scene in *Raiders of the Lost Ark* when Indiana Jones falls through a hole in the sand and lands in the Well of Souls, which is essentially a dark room full of snakes. ("I *hate* snakes, Jacques!") He has to get out, and the only way to do so is to walk ever so carefully through this slithering carpet of hissing vipers, cobras, and mambas. Every step is fraught with danger. He has no way of knowing what will set them off. The same was true for Sharon during her attempts to navigate around my moods.

Without putting too fine a point on it, I was a fucking mess, and if Sharon was suffering or worrying or thinking about going to live with her mother, I was too far under the weight of my own head to notice. Now, looking back, I don't know how she made it through. Sharon has given me almost everything that I value in this world: love, companionship, children, support, sex, and so on. If she could do something about the traffic, teach me how to fly, and agree to give me blow jobs while I watch hockey on TV, I'd nominate her for sainthood. (Wait. Do Jews believe in saints? Well, if we don't, I'd nominate her for God.) But aside from our kids, Sharon's greatest gift to me was simply that she hung in there with me through my darkest days. There has never in my life been a more powerful and resounding manifestation of love, and I will never again snicker when I hear a marrying couple recite the "in sickness and in health" line.

Still, she needed help. We both did, as individuals *and* as a married couple, and we agreed that such help could only come from psychotherapy. Through cryptic and highly secretive conversations with only our very closest friends, we dropped hints that we might be looking for a good shrink.

"You're going to call Susan," said Sharon's friend Jennifer. It was a declaration, not a suggestion. "You absolutely have to call her. She's awesome."

Awesome? Therapists aren't *awesome*. Therapists are subdued people in neutral-colored sweaters. Before I was able to independently verify Jennifer's assessment, I pictured Susan making an "awesome" entrance to the therapy session very much like a professional basketball player being introduced before a game, ripping off her snap-on warm-up pants and giving me a chest-bump as fireworks exploded over our heads. *And now! A five-foot-two, 115-pound therapist out of the Southern California School of Professional Psychology . . . Sssssssssusannnnn!* And the crowd goes wild. No. With therapists, the first several minutes of conversation are make or break. There is necessarily an element of trust that must be forged between shrink and client, and if the therapist gives even the slightest inclination that he or she doesn't "get" the client, the relationship is hosed. No one is going to reveal his deepest insecurities and phobias to someone who he believes to be an asshole.

"So what brings you in?" Susan asked. She sat on an ergonomically designed chair and rested her feet on a black plastic ergonomically correct platform. I could tell she was Jewish (it's a gift I have), and something about her tone and demeanor put me at ease. She was direct but not rude. She didn't fumble around for the right question like some of the other therapists I'd had; the conversation flowed naturally, as though we were old friends. That smoothness jibed with her appearance. A woman in her late fifties, there was no air of pretentiousness about her whatsoever. Beside her chair was a small, round table—the kind of place where one might normally place a framed photo of one's children or spouse. Susan had a photo of her horse.

Almost a full year after the lowest pit of my depression, several months after we'd started seeing Susan,

Sharon revealed in a joint therapy session that in the depths of her despair she'd called our friend Heather in Hawaii. Although it was only around eight thirty p.m., I was asleep. (This was one of the strangest of my symptoms. I could barely stay awake until eight.) And for the first time since I became ill, she shed her strength and stoicism and allowed herself to break down.

"I'm losing hope, Heather," she said, sobbing into the phone. "I have no idea how we're going to get out of this or how things can possibly get better any time soon. I don't want our kids to grow up in this environment."

Until that point, Sharon operated under the presumption that the best thing she could do for me to get better was get out of my way—to let me drink and sleep and cry and heal at my own pace and on my own terms. But over time my depression became an immobile generator of interference in our marriage, our parenthood, and even our ability to have a conversation with each other, and her mental health started to bear the brunt of its impact, too. She was breaking down. The snakes were sinking their fangs into her, and their venom was beginning to take hold.

She called Susan one morning during the very worst of it, hoping she might be able to schedule an appointment for that very day. She was lying in bed, crying, as she left a message on Susan's answering machine. The call was returned very shortly thereafter, and after an appointment was set for that afternoon, Sharon broke down again.

"Susan, am I totally screwed here?"

"This isn't the time to start making decisions about the future, Sharon. You can't. The best thing you can do for yourself right now is wait and see what Danny does. See how he responds."

EIGHT

had thumbed through two miserably outdated issues of *Entertainment Weekly* and a mind-numbing
brochure touting the myriad antioxidant benefits of
pomegranates when my gaunt, balding, children's-
charity-tie-wearing primary-care doctor sauntered
into examination room two.

"How's it going, Daniel?" he asked. I was under no
impression that he actually knew my name. He saw it
on my chart.

"I'm okay. How are you?"

"Better than you, from what I can tell," he said.

Clever. Asshole.

I said nothing. I just waited for him to start asking
the same question I have been asked during my first
visit to every primary-care doctor, therapist, and psy-

chiatrist I've seen in the past seven years. "Hi. How are you? Do you want to kill yourself? No? Good. Let's move on."

I didn't want to be there. I've hated going to the doctor since I was a child, because when I was nine, during a routine visit to the pediatrician's office in the mini-mall, next to Pick 'n Save, I was told that I had a hernia and an undescended testicle, and that I would need to have surgery to correct the problems because it would have been cruel for them to let me grow up thinking I had only one ball (which is, in fact, what I genuinely believed until that day at the doctor's office). I was petrified. An operation?! I'd seen a sufficient number of *Emergency!* episodes to know that when Johnny and Roy brought a mangled human in for surgery (which was after they'd followed orders to start an IV with D5W and transport as soon as possible), Dr. Brackett and Nurse Dixie started furrowing their brows and manning battle stations in the OR. It was serious shit. I didn't recall an episode where Squad 51 responded to a testicular emergency, but I assumed that I, just like the rescued suckers on *Emergency!*, would soon be on a stretcher having my vital signs monitored by some two-bit soap opera nurse while Dr. Brackett cut away my Garanimals and started inspecting my uni-ball.

So, no, I didn't want to be there in the doctor's office, even all those years later. More specifically, I didn't want what I had come to get from my doctor. I didn't want what I needed. Susan's recommendation that I obtain a prescription for antidepressant medication, while not terribly surprising given my circumstance, made me feel weak. I'd never before taken pills for anything other than a sinus infection. But as much as I wanted to puff out my chest and believe I could conquer my depression by sheer force of will, I knew that was an impossibility. I needed help, as shitty as that was, and only a doctor could give me what I needed— even a doctor in a bad tie.

Before he could begin doctoring, he looked up and gave me a once-over—the kind you might expect if you walked into a smoothie bar wearing nothing but a smile and a studded cock ring.

"Wow," he said. "That is a really nice shirt."

"Oh. Thanks," I said. "Eddie Bauer."

"Eddie Bauer, huh?" he said, tilting his head back slightly to look through the bottom of his bifocals. "That is a really, really nice shirt."

And with that my doctor walked over and began to feel my clothing—*while I was wearing it!* He grabbed a piece of the fabric on my sleeve between his thumb and forefinger and rolled it back and forth like a thumb-sucking toddler copping a touch-buzz from the ear of his teddy bear.

I was completely freaked out, but the little four-year-old inside of me thought if I didn't sit still I would have to get a shot and I really didn't want a shot because shots hurt and I'm not really good with pain. So I just sat there, staring straight ahead, letting the doctor get his jollies from my starched white Eddie

Bauer button-down shirt, which I vowed never to wear again.

"I don't think I've ever seen a shirt quite like this one," he said with a glassed-over look on his face. "It's so strong and firm. Very well constructed, you know what I mean?"

"Yeah," I said. "Strong. Firm."

(Kind of like the bottom of the Timberland hiking boot on my right foot, which is going straight up your ass if you don't *Back! The hell! Up!* Right now.)

I needed to change the subject immediately or face the very genuine possibility that my doctor was going to ask me to remove my underpants so he could commence his examination of my brain chemistry with a closer look at my testis satchel. I blurted out—in a moment of absolute heterosexual, woman-loving terror—"Do you, um, see many depressed men in your daily rounds?"

The glaze vanished from his eyes. I had performed the equivalent of walking in on him while he was having his way with the bearskin rug on the living room floor. He snapped out of his haze and, lo and behold, began to ask me if I'd ever thought of harming myself or if I heard voices no one else could hear.

The answer to the second question was yes; I heard a voice inside my head. It said, "Dude, get your prescription and run!"

The pharmacy near our house was built with a drive-thru, presumably because people like me would rather not walk in and risk having our prescriptions seen by people who would, you know, *tell.*

"*May I help you?*"

"Uh, yeah, I'm here to pick up a prescription for Evans."

"*First name?*"

"Danny. Uh, Daniel. Daniel."

Through the little speaker next to my driver's-side window I could hear the ruffling of paper and the rattle of filled prescription bottles bumping into each other. I always wonder what prescriptions are next to mine in that big drawer full of white paper bags, each one containing an amber bottle full of something. Who are my drawer mates? Is there another Evans? If so, what's his malady? Is he diabetic? Does he have cancer? What if it's a woman? Is she picking up her birth control? Does she have panic attacks or a yeast infection or osteoporosis? And who's the sickest person in the E drawer? Is it me? Shit, what if it *is* me?

"*Daniel Evans?*"

"Yes."

"*Can you confirm your date of birth for me, hun?*"

"Four twenty-nine seventy."

"*Okay, and have you taken this medication before, Mr. Evans?*"

"No."

"*Would you like to speak to the pharmacist?*"

"No."

"*Okay. I'm stapling a guide to taking this medication*

to your prescription. I encourage you to read it thoroughly and call your doctor if you have any questions."

"Okay."

"Will there be anything else?"

"No. Thanks."

She placed a white paper bag into the giant metal drawer beneath the window, then pushed a handle and sent the drawer yawning open toward me. I retrieved the bag, forced a smile at the cashier, and headed home.

A few moments later, I parked my Honda CR-V parallel with the curb in front of our house. After a deep breath, I opened the bag and pulled out the first of two tall, amber-shaded plastic bottles.

Sertraline (generic Zoloft), 50 mg. Take one tablet by mouth every day. May cause drowsiness. Taking this medicine alone or with alcohol may lessen your ability to drive or perform hazardous tasks.

I felt afraid. Ashamed. I knew what I held in my hand was a sign of weakness. A sign that I needed help. I hate needing help. I hate feeling as though I am not in control. I hate feeling like a pussy.

When I got into the house, I set the bottle down and detached from the envelope a four-page manifesto detailing how the accompanying medications should be taken (with food, at bedtime, with one eye closed, while clucking like a chicken), how it should *not* be taken (with alcohol, while breastfeeding, under water, in a communist country), and what has happened to other people who've taken it and might also happen to you. The second bottle, which contained a sleep aid, had its own manifesto, too, and although it was mostly the same as the sertraline, there was one additional word I'd never seen before: *priapism*.

The word sounded happy and chipper. I conjured images of fun and levity, like a child's birthday party. "Please join us this Sunday as we celebrate Timmy's rootin'est, tootin'est birthday party. We'll play Pin the Tail on the Donkey, eat Dippin' Dots, and enjoy a rousing game of *priapism*! Please RSVP, partner."

How fun! Hardly a potential side effect to worry about with a name like that, right?

I looked up the word.

PRIAPISM
pri • a • pism | [**prayh**-uh-piz-uhm]
—*noun* Persistent, often painful erection of the penis, *especially* as a consequence of disease and not related to sexual arousal.
—*origin* **Priapus:** Greek mythological character. A god of gardens and fertility, Priapus was the son of Aphrodite, who disowned him because he had a grotesque little body with a huge penis.

Wait. *What?!*

It had been years since I'd been tested for reading comprehension, but I was reasonably certain the message being sent was that taking these meds exposed me to a painful, useless, long-lasting boner named after a dead midget freak.

"Mom. Remember when you used to be a nurse?"

She chuckled into the phone. "Yes, I vaguely remember something like that."

"Okay, what's priapism?"

Laughter.

"No, I'm serious. What is it?"

"Why do you want to know?"

"Just *tell* me!"

"Watch your tone, mister. Okay. If I remember right, it's an erection that lasts a long time. And it hurts."

"Lovely. Thanks for nothing, Ma."

Click.

"Sharon?" I called out down the hall. "If you want some sex you'd better come and get it now because my dick might explode the second I take this pill!"

"Okay!" she shouted back. "Be right there! Just folding some laundry!"

A beat.

"Honey?"

"Yeah?"

"Would you still love me if I had a grotesque little body and a big old penis?"

"Probably not!" she yelled. "You'd remind me too much of my husband!"

Jews are big on ceremony.

When a baby boy is eight days old, we gather to

scarf corned beef and kugel while Rabbi Mordechai Ben Sadism ceremoniously mutilates the poor kid's wiener. *Mazel tov!* When that same boy is thirteen, we gather in the *shul* to witness the fruits of a year's worth of badgering ("Go practice your *haftorah!*") and guilt ("Your uncle Saul is flying all the way from Skokie for your Bar Mitzvah, Daniel. Do you want him to see you behaving like a *schmendrik*?). *Mazel tov!* There are Hebrew blessings that turn even the most mundane of human behaviors—washing hands, eating a peach, setting your TiVo to record the season premiere of *So You Think You Can Yodel*—into low-grade ceremony. You took a crap? *Mazel tov! Blessed are you, O Lord Our God, King of the Universe, who made my exit door in such a way that I was able to pass that huge carne asada burrito without the use of a shoehorn. Amen.*

Given our penchant for turning nothing into something, I felt compelled—almost mandated—to make a spectacle out of taking my first antidepressant pill. This was a big deal to me. As the manifesto foretold, there was no way of knowing what swallowing that little white dot would do to me.

. . . *and in some cases, death.*

I grabbed a bottle of water from the fridge and sat down on the couch next to Sharon. Noah was crashing a toy car into the living room baseboards.

"Okay, guys," I said. "Here goes. . . ."

Swallow.

I sat for a moment and wallowed in my own anticipation. I expected an immediate reaction. A spontaneous panic attack. A dizzy spell. A painful erection.

"Well?" Sharon asked.

"Nothing. Not a damn thing. Maybe it's a placebo."

Noah hit the wall with his car again. Sharon got up to answer the telephone, leaving me alone on the couch with my water, my bottle of pills, and my dread. I was certain that my life was changing but I couldn't see how. Could a pill really rescue me? I convinced myself that it could, and then I waited.

NINE

Persistent dizziness was the only noticeable change after two weeks on the medication. I still felt depressed, even more so when I discovered that the drug that was supposed to undepress me was a dud. Or maybe the meds *were* as potent as people said they are and the problem was that my depression was somehow unique and untreatable with pedestrian pharmaceuticals. That had to be it. My depression was "special."

Since I couldn't sleep, either, I wiggled out of bed early one morning and consulted the Internet for information about how I *should* have been feeling. I spent hours trolling the Antidepressant Side Effects message boards in search of someone else suffering from this drug-resistant strain of depression. I found no such confirmation. In fact, the messages fell into one of two distinct categories:

1. Antidepressants are miracle drugs.

"OMG! I got really super duper depressed after my boyfriend broke the TiVo and I missed a whole week of *The Young and the Restless* (I *LOVE* Jack!). My sykyitrist put me on auntie-depressints and alls I can say is that this shit totally works. LOL! I had some dry mouth at first and I was dizzy a lot and my head hurted, but it has been a munth now and I feel rad. I *LOVE* my meds! But not as much as I love Jack. ROFLMFAO!"

2. Antidepressants are a wretched curse upon mankind.

"I don't know what they put in this crap but it shortened my temper to where I would black out and get extremely violent. Several people I know who took this medication experienced the same side effect. After about two months of using the drugs, I blacked out and beat the shit out of my boss, who is also my mother. The other violent episodes only involved dishes, walls and this one kid at the food court in the mall who was eyeballing my Sbarro."

Reading the caustic descriptions of symptoms and doomsday predictions, I noticed that many of the reviews suggested herbal and homeopathic remedies that, as was the common vernacular, "promote mental wellness." Given that my first prescription was so far entirely nonbeneficial, I decided to jot down a few of the remedies referenced and check them out at the health food store. I found each potion from my list on the shelves but there was no differentiable information from one bottle to the next. Turns out the FDA doesn't want the manufacturers of these puppies to claim they're a "cure," so the language on the labels says virtually nothing of substance. And what could one possibly infer from the line drawing of an herb leaf, which showed up on the front of each plastic bottle?

I decided then to choose my herb the same way I chose my woman: which one looked the least intimidating? Saint-John's-wort had sharp edges. SAM-e looked like aliens distributed it. Valerian root reminded me too much of this girl Valerie I knew in elementary school. She put gum on my chair.

The winner of the herbal remedy beauty contest was 5-HTP. The bottle had a bright yellow sun on the front. And I liked the name; if 1-HTP was good then five of them had to be pretty damn good. I wondered what HTP stood for. **H**ide **T**he **P**enis. **H**ave **T**his **P**ickled. **H**ow's **T**he **P**latypus? I brought the bottle home, fished through the yards and yards of cotton and pulled out one pill. Looked pretty standard. I swallowed it with a gulp of orange Gatorade.

That night I woke up in a pile of my own shit.

Hate **T**hese **P**ills.

For the second time in my life, I regretted not believing in Gee-Dash-Dee. It would have been so convenient to be able to pray for relief, to request a path back to myself from something that could deliver it, to have a reason to believe someone with a lot of pull was looking out for me. *Blessed are you, O Lord, King of the Universe, Who will get on the horn with my doctor and make him make me better or else face the consequence of bunking with Hitler for all eternity. Amen.*

I couldn't. I don't pray. I realized years earlier when we had a miscarriage that "believing" only at the lowest points of one's life was hypocritical and just plain dumb. It would have been preposterous to start talking to Gee-Dash-Dee and asking Him for favors only in times of desperation and anguish. I had no option but to endure. If I wanted to believe in something, the only choice was to believe that I would heal, that I would someday escape the thick fog that had enveloped my spirit, my soul, my lust for life. I felt naked. Raw. I was left to continue stabbing at the dark in search of relief from what felt like my life disintegrating against my will.

There was a bright side, though. After two weeks, my penis still had not exploded.

If depression has even one redeeming quality, it's that it strong-arms its victims into a mode of intense self-analysis. One flatly cannot pull himself out of the pit of self-hatred and despair until he makes the effort to understand why he feels this way. Fortunately for some of us, we learn other valuable things about ourselves along the way. For example, I learned that sometimes sex isn't about love or procreation or connectedness; it's about getting off. Sharon understood this about me before I did, and given that she was unable to connect with me in any emotional way, she dutifully obliged my primal need to take my pants off and control something in a way that married men don't usually get to control unless they get a raise, bring home flowers, or do the laundry without being asked.

We had been doing it for over an hour already—a new team record—and I wasn't even close to . . . you know . . . *deploying*. We were exhausted. I was confused. Frustrated. Tired. My attempt to get off had inexplicably become a marathon, and my stamina was beginning to wither. I tried to go faster, then slower. I was on top, then bottom. There was saliva and sweat and synthetic substances everywhere. These were the same conditions in which we'd engaged in legally sanctioned matrimonial interaction hundreds of times before, but this time Colonel Creamaster declined to cooperate.

"I'm sorry, honey," I said. "I have no idea what's happening here."

"You don't have to apologize," she said.

(As someone who had until recently made his living in advertising, I subconsciously stored that line away in hopes that I would someday be summoned to write a slogan for an erectile dysfunction treatment. *Dick Medicine™. Because you shouldn't have to apologize.*)

"Do you want me to rub it?" she asked.

"Worth a try, I guess."

I assumed the position and we began. Gobs and gobs of KY. One hand. Two hands. Left hand. Right. Rub rub rub. For twenty minutes.

Nothing.

Slower. Faster. Smack it. Spit on it. Stick something in my ass. Sing me show tunes.

Nothing.

"Am I doing something wrong?" Sharon asked.

"No. It feels awesome. I just . . . I don't know."

Defeated, I declared the moment over and released my wife to her hard-earned slumber. I got up to go to the bathroom with a penis that looked and felt as though it had just gone twelve brutal rounds with a rolling pin. I sat down on the toilet lid and buried my head in my hands. What had become of me? Even during the times when I held very little control over my own future, my penis and my sexuality (or lack thereof) were entirely mine. When there was rejection and sadness and loneliness, I could find a measure of solace in locking myself in a room, biting my lip, closing my eyes, and imagining that Farrah Fawcett or Kate Smith or Julie the Cruise Director from *The Love Boat* couldn't get enough of me. *I* decided which actress to nail and in which position and where the goo would go. But now that control was gone, and with it went a sense of my manhood. I was powerless. But how? Why?

I opened a drawer under the bathroom sink and retrieved the four-page manifesto that was stapled to my antidepressant prescription. And there it was, right between blurred vision and skin rash.

Delayed ejaculation.

Hate **T**he **P**enis.

TEN

Of course there was also the issue of my penis. Beyond the obvious emotional and physical toll of the disease, a diagnosis of depression challenged the conventional behaviors that made me a Man. I naively believed my *shvantz* was a built-in anti-venin for emotion. I believed in my blissful ignorance that depression was reserved for overwhelmed, post-partum moms and troubled teenage girls and under-appreciated stay-at-home moms who need "mother's little helper" to ferry them through their daily monotony. But a clinically depressed *dude*? No way, man. Not me. I'm no pussy. I play hockey. I have sex *all the time*. With a woman! But that's the thing about depression—even though you can't see it and you refuse to believe it has thrust its talons into you, the fight ends quickly. Mine did. I succumbed and started to live *inside* of depression, as though it was a thin coating that surrounded my entire existence like the layer of congealed yuck that forms over the gravy on Thanksgiving Day. The world became gray and muted. What once gave me joy and self-worth withered into nuisance, as though I had somehow become allergic to everything but sadness and numbness. There were days when life itself was a plague, when leaving the bedroom was out of the question, when a chore as rudimentary as walking to the bathroom felt like running a marathon in cement shoes. I wanted to be angry. I wanted to resist, to get up, get dressed, and go to work, but I was powerless to do so. I wanted to assure my wife and son that whatever was happening to me was only temporary, like a cold or chicken pox. But that was my brave face talking. That was me trying to hold on to traditional Manhood. The truth was I couldn't feel much at all, and I was scared.

As a boy, I played with toys that looked like Superman and Luke Skywalker, not little action figures of Woody Allen. I learned by watching *CHiPs* and *S.W.A.T.* and the cigarette commercials in between that men are stoic, rugged, and emotionless. We ignore pain. In the school yard, the boys who performed poorly in sports were labeled "pussy" or "sissy"—words intended to convey femininity, and therefore weakness. (Ironically, it's that very stigma of male invulnerability that makes us so prone to depression—the ultimate emasculating diagnosis.) I believed all of it. Then, when I turned thirty, it all went to shit. We are not emotionless, robotic beings; we are entirely fallible and completely human. We feel sadness, sorrow, fear, angst—but we resist it. It's shameful. But I couldn't help it. I knew it wasn't normal for a dude to put his emotions and their effect on his life on display because those were the behavioral manifestations assigned to women. In fact some of us—myself included—*never* feel compelled to expose (or even recognize) feelings of hurt and pain until we have sunken so low that we have no other choice. It's in our nature to hide from sadness, and many men do so through compulsiveness and self-destructive analgesics. Some of us redirect ourselves with work, which keeps us from exposing our pain to friends and family simply by being in their presence. Other guys bury their depression under alcohol, drugs, adultery, gambling, and other risky, reckless diversions. At the height of my depression, I was guilty of some of those crimes against myself. I knew what I was doing; depression short-circuited my mood, not my intellect. I was aware that I was drinking too much and staring into the computer monitor too long and going to bed at seven thirty so frequently that I was not even present to portray the model of a father, let alone a respectable one. But I was powerless to change it.

I stopped caring what people thought. I didn't care who knew I had a mental illness because I was numb, and nothing anyone could say could have feasibly made things worse. So I opened the floodgates and started yapping.

"So, how ya been, Danny?"

"Eh. I've been better."

"Why? What's wrong?"

"I have depression, Bob."

"Oh. Uh. Sorry, man. Anything I can do for you?"

"Actually, yes. Sit down and let me tell you about my childhood."

"I . . . uh . . . I . . ."

"Don't fuck with me, Bob. I'm in a really bad place right now and I really don't want to have to cut you."

3 . . . 2 . . . 1 . . .

I surrender with a smile. "Relax, Bobby. I'm just playing with you. I'm fine."

That part was the real lie. I wasn't fine. But the trouble with talking about depression was that nobody knew how to react, or maybe it was just that I didn't know what kind of reaction I wanted from them. It's easier to blame it on someone else, especially when you can see them searching for the words, scanning their memories for the appropriately sensitive reaction while simultaneously wondering what it means to be depressed and whether the revelation that I suffered from a mental illness somehow put them at risk. Was I suicidal? Was I going to freak out? I knew these fears because I experienced them myself, but I also knew what it looks like from the other side and it struck me to see otherwise wonderful people flailing this way when they heard the word "depression." As grueling as it was to experience depression, doing so in the omnipresence of social stigma and ignorance that surround the disease made the task of recovery exponentially harder. People seemed to have an expectation that happiness and contentment can be turned off and on like a faucet, that all I needed to do was decide not to be depressed and I'd be better. Their confusion confused me, too. Maybe they were right. Maybe I was just being a puss.

I went to therapy to save my marriage and my relationship with my child, and I began to talk more about my depression as the cloud began to dissipate. Talking about it brought out of the woodwork other men— friends of mine—who had encountered the disease. I'd known some of these guys for a decade or longer, but I was unaware that they had suffered like I did. When I began to share my story with them, it was as though an imaginary dam had sprung a leak of pure emotion—feelings kept within an impenetrable containment, lest they flood the community with realities too raw to accept, too real to cast aside with a "hang in there" or a "suck it up, buddy." A corporate vice president, a deputy district attorney, a salesman—men of different races, different socioeconomic strata, all bound together by a disease and the common belief that no one else understands what they're going through. But I did.

Depression was potent enough to transform me, a committed husband and new father, into an isolated, perverted, joyless menace. I gathered up as much beer and porn and anger as I could, and with it I built a wall around myself. No one could get into my fortress, not even my wife or our baby boy.

Once I was able to calm my friends down and assure them that I wasn't going to kill them, they asked me how it feels to be depressed, and this is what I told them:

Depression feels like the physiological equivalent of the shamefully overedited porn they show in hotel rooms. In each case there is obviously *something* unsavory going on—something that manifests with facial contortions and heaving chests and lots of grunting—but you can't definitively identify it. That's partly why I had so much trouble believing I was depressed: there was no visual manifestation of it. They call it a disease but there is no tangible evidence of its existence. Other diseases can be *seen*. A rogue white dot on an X-ray. A dramatic change in weight or complexion. A printed lab report replete with sinister figures and disquieting statistical conclusions. But there is no such thing with mental illnesses. There's nothing to blame them on, nothing to hold in your hands and rage against in moments of hopelessness and despair. Depression exists only because you know it's there, like Gee-Dash-Dee and MSG and the Force.

From an engineering point of view, depression is a stunning achievement. Its effect burrows into the fabric of its victim, sparing nothing as it draws an otherwise happy person back into himself, enforcing the impression that he is a passenger in his own body. He is isolated, lost inside his own mind. Concentration shuts down. Reason and logic evaporate. Life becomes unrelenting drudgery—physically, mentally, spiritually, emotionally. He is left with little else but disorientation and fear.

I was beginning to see why people kill themselves. Life with depression isn't life at all; it's mere existence. We are programmed throughout our lives that nothing worthwhile comes easy, and that is certainly true of recovery, of ascent from the depths. Sometimes the prospect of living that way for even an hour longer presents such a viscerally repulsive scenario that death seems like an easier option. Survival takes too long; it's a commitment with an indefinite timeline. Death is immediate and permanent. It's relief. And to a person whose ability to make decisions is essentially paralyzed, the nerve it takes to choose life over death can't always be summoned.

I never made an attempt, never even seriously considered taking myself out of the game, but the concept made sense to me. On nights when sleep was fleeting (if even present at all), my mind wandered into that domain. What if the situation deteriorated? How would I do it? Pills? Nah, too passive. I once looked into the medicine cabinet to see if there was anything that might do the job, but I don't believe there has ever been a successful suicide attempt using the lethal cocktail of Tums, Imodium, and chewable vitamins. How 'bout a train? Might hurt innocent people. I stopped there. I convinced myself that I was just too chickenshit to take myself out in a blaze of glory; I'm not a fan of pain. And every time I let myself dip a toe in those muddied waters, I saw the faces of my wife and child, and that immediately yanked me back to emotional sobriety. A virtual ice bath. Recovery was my only option. If it meant spending the rest of my life in an institution, at least I'd be alive. At least I'd still have the eyes to see them, the arms to hug them, the heart to love them. And when it came down to it, my need to love them, and my need to have them love me, were stronger than the fear. The way Sharon reaches down and grabs my hand under the covers when she wakes up in the morning. Noah's hope-filled blue eyes. That was my life. That was why I needed to live, why I needed to eliminate any option but recovery.

I bought a lot of books about depression, figuring that by taking an intellectual approach to the disease I could get inside the disease's head. I would outsmart it. I would learn what made it tick, find out where it liked to hang out, stake it out, and then leap out of the shadows and crack it over the head with a pipe wrench. Unfortunately, reading comprehension is a virtual impossibility in the depressed mind. I forgot what I'd read before I'd even finished the paragraph. I also bought Sharon a book: *When Someone You Love Is Depressed.* In retrospect, this seemingly innocuous gesture was emblematic of the problem that threatened our marriage most during my illness: I didn't communicate with my wife. I can't say whether I was incapable of doing so or just too lethargic to really care, but she was left in the dark about what I was thinking and how I was feeling. That's why I passive-aggressively bought the book for her; if I couldn't/wouldn't tell her what was going on, maybe this author could. I needed Sharon to understand what I could not tell her myself. Maybe the author could act as my proxy, my mouthpiece, and sit down with my wife over a cup of Earl Grey, explain to her that I wasn't really in control of myself anymore, and tell her not to take my buffoonery personally. "There, there, dear," it would say.

I have wondered to myself what I would have done if our roles were reversed—if *she* was the spouse who was clinically depressed. If *she* was the spouse who isolated herself, who left the entirety of the familial responsibilities to me, who shut down and shielded herself with alcohol and porn and isolation. How long could I have taken that? How much would I have put up with before I left the house? How far can empathy and love sustain you before the instincts for survival and guardianship compel a person to make the decision to break free?

ELEVEN

I met with and "interviewed" six different therapists—endeavoring with each one to find a comfortable measure of connection and a general sense that the shrink "got me"—and every single one of them had an ugly couch. I don't mean the kind of ugly you'd see on a frat house couch, where legions of drunken general studies majors have offloaded enough spilled Coors Light, Copenhagen spit, and errant semen to give the faux leather sectional a glossy sheen. I mean the kind of ugly you'd see if you walked in on the chubby, hopelessly single cat lover next door at two in the morning and caught her in the size XXL muumuu she bought on QVC. Although I have no formal training in psychology or psychiatry or any of the other head-shrinking arts, I've seen enough circumstantial evidence to believe the presence of abhorrent furnishings is a tool therapists use to effectually blind their patients, thereby forcing them to close their eyes and look inside their souls.

Susan was recommended so highly by a good friend that I just had to go in and see her, if only once, if only just to see if there's such a thing as a "superstar" therapist. Her small office was tucked away on the second floor of a large corporate office park. I opened the door to suite 201 to find a miniaturized version of a typical therapist waiting room: weathered secondhand wicker furniture, a small coffeepot with a collection of ceramic mugs and powdered condiments, and a table littered with expired issues of *Psychology Today*, *Psychotherapy Networker*, and a rogue, out-of-place issue of *Car and Driver*. There were white streaks on the cover of the latter, remnants of a hastily stripped mailing label. I assumed that meant somebody left the magazine behind after a visit and Susan didn't want to add to her library by violating someone's HIPAA rights. I sat down, considered reading, but instead chose to sit back and fold my hands in my lap. A moment later, a side door opened.

"Daniel?" the woman asked.

"Susan?"

"Yes. Hi. Please, come on in."

I was invited to make myself comfortable on a love seat upholstered with a repugnant floral print fabric that, had I not been so emotionally stupefied at the time, would have motivated me to set my hair on fire and run screaming from the building. Even in the shadows of framed artwork that appeared to have been looted from a Motel 6 and two mammoth bookcases filled with obscure psychological texts like *How to Talk to Your Co-Dependant Transgender Teenager About Spontaneous Menopause*, the couch was the room's dominant eyesore. It looked like a palm tree had puked on it.

Susan sat across from me in a black leather chair and rested her stocking- and sandal-clad feet on an angled, ergonomically correct platform that made me want to go skateboarding. A cup of tea rested on a small table to her right, next to the picture of a horse, and the absence of rising steam told me it had been there for a session or two.

"Have you had thoughts of harming yourself?" she asked through a moderate New York accent that turned the word "thoughts" into something like "thow-watts."

"No."

She checked a box on her clipboard. (I can make the argument that the mental health community uses more clipboards than any other business sector. All shrinks should be born with a thin, flat piece of black plastic in their thighs and a hoo-hah that clamps down on paper.)

"When you go to sleep, do you often wish you would not wake up?"

"No."

Check.

"Do you hear voices that no one else can hear?"

"Pfft."

She looked up from the clipboard and registered my disgust. "Sorry," she said. "I know these questions can sound a little strange but I have to ask them. Just a few more, okay?"

"Okay."

I rate the awkwardness of the first session with a new therapist on par with having a prostate examination. In each case one is intentionally poked and prodded in an area not normally prone to such focused attention. There exists at the beginning of each experience a sort of "feeling-out" process. How deep is too deep? How open is the patient willing to be? How will he react when tender areas are touched? The discomfort in the room is enormous and gauche, but it goes unspoken because both the examiner and the examinee know it just has to be done. And when it's over one is left with a disconcerting personal quandary: *Did I just enjoy that?*

"Have you experienced any major life changes in the last year? Have you moved or changed jobs or lost someone close to you . . . ?"

"I became a father," I said. "Then, about a month ago, I got laid off. And 9/11 happened four days later."

She must have heard the pain in my voice or seen it on my face because she leaned forward, hands clasped, and looked at me for an uncomfortable, silent moment. I felt like one of the live lobsters at the seafood counter in the grocery store, being studied by someone whose only interest was to crack me open and get at my insides.

"Tell me how you feel," she said.

A long pause.

"I feel numb."

The room smelled like rain, and the hole-pocked foam ceiling panels were dotted with stains from the brown water bleeding down from a leaky metal roof. It felt oddly appropriate to be sitting under the collateral damage from a downpour. My mind recalled the image of the sad little egg in the Zoloft commercials that has a rain cloud gushing down on him wherever he goes. (Although to my knowledge eggs can't actually move voluntarily.)

Susan said nothing in response to my declaration. She engaged "the silent treatment" technique, which I remembered from my days as a newspaper reporter: when the person to whom you are speaking hasn't said enough, just look at him without saying a word. The focused attention makes people uncomfortable and their nervous reaction is to speak, if only to break the unbearable silence.*

_____

* I once tried to employ this technique in an interview with Tiger Woods. He was home in Southern California from Stanford for the Thanksgiving vacation and I was commissioned to write a feature story about him. Although he was not yet a pro (and therefore didn't yet have a Gatorade named after him), it was clear to those who followed golf that he would soon turn the sport on its ass. Tiger was picking the bell peppers out of his Denver omelet when I asked him some lame question about

"Just a minute ago I was waiting at a red light over on Jamboree Road and I started to cry. But there was no reason for it. I wasn't in pain or anything. Nothing bad happened. I just started crying, out of the blue."

"That's the depression," she said sympathetically.

The word seemed like an insult. An accusation. I knew little about mental illness—only what I'd seen in *One Flew Over the Cuckoo's Nest*—but I knew enough to believe Susan was dead wrong. Depression = crazy. Crazy = people who mutter angrily to themselves, people who see things that aren't really there, people who try to kill themselves. Crazy doesn't = me. I'm married + I have a son + I have a *college degree*, for Pete's sake! These things > crazy. Crazy most certainly does *not* = me.

I would like to tell you that I said these things aloud to Susan, but I didn't. I merely sat there on the offensively upholstered floral couch, sunk into myself, and began to wonder what had happened to my life.

---

something unimportant. Thirty seconds passed and still no answer. I tried to wait him out, but I blinked first and asked him something else. And suddenly I knew how it felt to be Phil Mickelson.

TWELVE

believed I had taken depression's best punch. It staggered me and bloodied my nose, but it certainly hadn't knocked me down. I assumed it couldn't get any worse than what I felt in the first few weeks of the fight, but boy was I wrong. I had no concept of how bad it could get, and because I was already in therapy, already taking pills, already trying to stop the bleeding, I never saw the knockout punch coming.

I was facedown on the California King–sized mattress we bought on the cheap when we got married. I pulled the covers over my head and buried my face so completely in my pillow that I could smell the scent of my own dried drool. It was two thirty in the afternoon and all I wanted to do was disappear. I wanted the linens to swallow me whole. I wanted the mattress to fold over me like a taco shell—to wrap me up in a cocoon of springs and synthetic foam and protect me. But that wouldn't make much sense, would it? It wouldn't make sense because what I wanted to be protected from was inside my head. I could not hide from it any more than I could hide from the blue in my eyes. Still, this was the only place I could be. In the dark. In the quiet. Away from the irritants of movement and voice and life.

It's a miserable way to exist, and no retreat is far enough away from the fray to escape. You're locked inside your own head.

I went to Las Vegas with a buddy when we were twenty-two years old, the plan being to stay drunk and awake for the entire weekend and to see as many bare breasts as our meager incomes from the magic shop on Topanga Canyon would permit. (If they accepted card and coin tricks as payment on the Strip, we would have been the toast of the town.) An hour or so before we were going to see a show at the Imperial Palace—a parade of celebrity impersonators and topless show-girls with feathers on their heads—my buddy Andy opened his palm and revealed two small, square pieces of ivory-colored paper. It was LSD. Acid. I had never seen it before, but I knew what it was. I took one of the pieces, set it on the middle of my tongue, and waited for it to seep into my bloodstream. Thirty min-utes later I was locked in a bathroom stall at the IP, about 84 percent certain that I was going to die. My heart was racing. I was covered in sweat. Everything was spinning. I stayed in that stall for two hours, vacillating manically between dread that I was going to die in a bathroom at the most disgusting hotel on the Strip and low-grade pride that I was going to die the same way Jimi Hendrix did.

At times depression feels like that bad acid trip, but with a few notable differences. A bad trip wears off; depression doesn't. As bad as it is, you *know* a bad trip will eventually be over so you can get back to feeling like a normal human being (and, as was the case for me, soberly swearing that I will never go near that shit again). Depression does not come standard with any such optimism. In fact, lying facedown on the bed that afternoon, I felt the opposite of optimism. I felt dread. I felt horror. I convinced myself that I was destined to spend the rest of my days in a mental institution, and I began to imagine how that might look.

Although I grew up a short drive from the loony bin believed by some audiophiles to have been the inspiration for the Eagles' "Hotel California," I have never seen the inside of a psych ward. My points of reference were movies that featured big-time Hollywood celebrities acting like they are "disturbed." Jack Nicholson spiritedly and passionately calling the play-by-play action of an imaginary baseball game in the aforementioned *Cuckoo's Nest*. Angelina Jolie and Winona Ryder talking about slitting their wrists in *Girl, Interrupted*. Brad Pitt spewing all kinds of craziness but sounding moderately wise in *12 Monkeys*. This was my destiny. I would bunk with someone who flings his own shit at the walls. I would eat meals and endure group therapy with people who believe aliens from faraway planets are monitoring our thoughts. Perhaps I would soon say and do and think the same things. Perhaps I was only beginning to go crazy.

The more I considered these possibilities, the less far-fetched they became. But I could not escape them. They were inside me. They were the bad trip that never goes away.

Convinced that primary-care doctors knew as much about psychotropic medications as they do about the mating rituals of the southeast Norwegian Gila monster, Susan suggested I find myself a psychiatrist. I was frightened by the word, to say nothing of the actual experience. I pictured someone asking me to lie down on an ugly couch and talk about my oral fixations and my feelings about communism and my earliest memories of my mama.

I learned quickly that one of the great things about mental illness is the semiregular opportunity it gives a sufferer to sit in a psychiatrist's waiting room and attempt to decipher whether the other patients are more or less cuckoo than he. One imagines this is not the kind of game people with other illnesses and ailments play. Would a man waiting to see his cardiologist scan the waiting room, wondering if perhaps the old guy across the room has a more life-threatening arterial blockage than his? Do women waiting for their electrolysis appointments try to see if the other ladies in the room have fuller mustaches? Doubtful. But when you're loony, it's a comfort to know (or at least believe) that others in the room rank higher on the Nutjob Scale than you do.

The first time I walked into a psychiatrist's office I expected to find people banging their heads against the drywall or arguing the merits of menthol cigarettes with a potted ficus or channeling Jack Nicholson to the receptionist: *"Put your hand in the air, Chief! Don't you watch the ball game, Chief?"* Sadly, it was far less entertaining than that. No one spoke. No one displayed even a borderline sign of psychosis. In fact, the only real crazy person I saw that day was the psychiatrist himself—a balding, sweater-wearing old man who spoke in barely audible whispers. I called him Dr. Flatline.

The popular belief in the mental health community is that people who pursue a career in therapy or psychiatry do so partially because they wish to heal themselves. I think that sounds perfectly logical and justifiable. In the words of Public Enemy, "you gotta go with what you know," and a fair sampling of mental health professionals know how to be cuckoo. When one is in training to become a therapist, he *must* be in therapy himself, so the intuitive leap is that you have to learn what makes *you* nuts before you can help *others* who are nuts. Yet regardless of one's vocation, one can never completely stop being nuts, and anyone who disagrees would surely change his mind after spending five minutes in Dr. Flatline's dank, unkempt office.

The place smelled like a dead cat. The administrative staff was composed of gothed-out high school girls with black nail polish, black makeup, and a demeanor that led me to suspect one of them had found the key to the Valium sample stash. And because Dr. Flatline saw fit to treat adults and children in the same office suite, any attempt to read one of the outdated magazines in the waiting room was interrupted by the sound of a large plastic block chucked wildly across the room by the berserk little kid who was most certainly back to get a refill on the meds that keep her from acting like a syphilis-infected orangutan in full estrus. Indeed, you had to be crazy to go anywhere near Dr. Flatline. And of course, the situation only deteriorated when I was escorted back to his office.

He asked the questions—"Do you experience magical thinking that influences your behavior?" "Do you often hear voices that no one else can hear?"—and I was left to wonder if his inquiries were for clinical purposes or if he was just trying to find someone like himself. He appeared to be under the influence of every downer in the "candy drawer." And it got worse from there.

Red flag #1: I saw him three times and he never once made eye contact with me. I could have strolled in wearing a chicken costume and he never would have known.

Red flag #2: The man looked like a catatonic Mister Rogers. Same age. Same general appearance. He wore a brown button-down sweater, slip-on slippers, and that odd thousand-mile stare that gives you no choice but to wonder what secrets he harbors under all of that cat hair.

Red flag #3: I was under the impression that a licensed psychiatrist would make an attempt to understand my mental predicament before prescribing pills to treat it. But with Dr. Flatline, the prescription pad came out and the scripts started flying around the room like, well, like the large plastic blocks in the waiting room. *Want some Zoloft? Here, have some Zoloft! Have some Prozac and some Wellbutrin and some of those cool little green pills that make you fly! Have it all! Pills! Pills! Wheeeee! What? A second opinion? Phooey! Second opinions are for people who don't have any Xanax. Here, have some Xanax! Wheeeee!*

As I left his office for the last time, I did actually hear a voice no one else could hear. The voice wondered how long I would have to take all of these pills before I ended up brain-dead like Dr. Flatline.

My second psychiatrist, Dr. Nima, was a man of Middle Eastern descent, and my first impression of him was quite wonderful, although that had nothing to do with him. It was his receptionist, Emily, and her spectacular breasts. She was seated at her desk the first time I walked in, and although I am happily married to a gorgeous woman, it was impossible to look at anything other than her blouse (rather, the virtual lack thereof). There was nary a stitch of fabric between her collarbones and the area just above her nipples, and her boobs were so tightly wedged into their lacy harness as to look like a king-sized mattress stuffed into a sausage casing. (Have you ever heard a bra scream?) Emily had a lovely smile, which she showed me the first time I walked in and announced that I had come for my appointment. She spoke, and her response was about what you would expect from a woman like that in the presence of a waiting room full of mental cases. She handed me a clipboard and asked me to complete the standard forms it held, but she did so in a practiced, polished, professional tone that seemed to say, "If you're severely disturbed and homicidal, I hope my smoky voice, my intoxicating perfume, and this point-blank visual examination of my voluptuous boobies will convince you to walk away and kill someone besides me."

Dr. Nima's office sat at the end of a long hallway on the first floor of an office complex that straddled the border of two of Orange County's most affluent communities (neither of which I lived in). Closer to the front entrance is a mortgage company for which Sharon and her brother David once worked. I visited Sharon often when she worked in that office and I was certain there was someone there who would recognize me if they saw me through the enormous windows that separated the office from the entrance to the building. Great anxiety washed over me when I realized that someone, anyone, might see me walk in and follow me with their eyes as I strode down the hallway and into the office of a psychiatrist—a revelation from which any normal human being can determine that I'm crazy, and probably a menace to society, and that I will probably return at this time next week to kill everyone in the building with a ball-peen hammer. Then I'd make a soup with their chopped-up guts and slurp it down with some fava beans and a nice key-AN-tee. *Thipthip-thipthipthip.*

From my seat in the bright, spacious waiting room, I could see Emily's fire engine red G-string underwear peeking out from the waistband of her hooker jeans, perfectly underscoring the colorful but nondescript "tramp stamp" tattoo at the intersection of her spine and pelvis. I was falling in lust with Emily. The tits, the thong, the tat—she was Angelina Jolie without the prima donna attitude or the wedding ring—and my visits to Dr. Nima's office were regularly followed by a private moment at home with a bottle of Jergens lotion and a hand towel. Despite the display of pharmaceutical propaganda scattered throughout the room, each different brochure promising in pastel-colored headlines that the pills it promoted could help me get back to being the real me, I've never taken a pill that could do for me what the image of Emily, me, and a canister of Easy Cheese did.

Given the well-to-do location of Dr. Nima's office, he seemed to attract a more affluent mix of crazies. That made visits doubly fun for me. When I wasn't imagining myself taking target practice on Emily's tramp stamp, I incessantly deconstructed the white-collar psychos in the waiting room, projecting various ailments and lifestyles onto them. It made me feel better about myself to imagine the other freaks and kooks in the room were stewing a higher degree of wacko than I.

There's a woman with a Magnum P.I. *mustache sitting next to the magazine rack. See her? Don't make direct eye contact with her. She's here seeking treatment for a unique behavioral disorder called Manic Free-Range Poultry Associative Behavior. Whenever someone says the word "chicken," she tucks her hands under her armpits like wings and begins to cluck. "Buh-kawk! Buk-buk-buh-kawk!" Such a sad, misunderstood chickenwoman. Glad I'm not that sick.*

I expected the inside of a psychiatrist's office would look like it does in the movies: open, minimalist, a comfy leather couch perhaps. I mean, when you see the workspaces occupied by the shrinks on TV—like Dr. What's-Her-Name on *The Sopranos*—the neatness and order seem representative of a nasty case of OCD. Everything is "just so." But it was quite clear the moment I walked into his office that he was neither obsessive nor compulsive. But there was obviously some sort of disorder involved, as evidenced by the rampant . . . disorder. It looked like a blast zone. There were stacks of patient file folders on the floor, in the corners, and teetering on one side of his desk. Large textbooks peppered the area, many of them left open, relics of some past important search for comorbidity* or definition or treatment criterion. And if anyone ever decides to build a museum dedicated to those cheap plastic pens emblazoned with the logos of various pharmaceutical companies and their products, I suggest you start in Dr. Nima's office—but make sure you've had all of your shots first.

"Tell me, what brought you in today?" he said.

"Well, I was diagnosed with depression a few months ago and I've been getting my medication from my primary-care doctor until now," I said. "I'm beginning to believe he knows very little about mental health and I thought you could handle my situation more deftly."

"Yes," he said. "It has been my experience that primary-care physicians receive only a modicum of ed-yoo-cay-shun about treatment of depression and an-ex-aye-it-eee. I think I can help. Can you tell me what med-eee-cay-shuns you are taking right now, Mr. Eee-vans?"

"Zoloft. Twenty-five milligrams."

"And how have you been feeling?"

"Not great," I said. "It was working well at one time but lately I've felt like my body is developing a tolerance for it."

---

* Two diseases that occur together, such as anxiety and depression.

"Do you mean some of your depressive symptoms have gotten stronger?"

"Yes."

"Give me an example of how this feels."

I thought for a moment. A deep breath.

"I get these strange little zaps in my head," I said.

He looked perplexed. "Zaps? What do you mean by zaps?"

"It's hard to explain. I feel very short bursts of something in my brain, like an electrical impulse or a jolt of energy. It lasts only a split second but it can be pretty distracting."

It wasn't registering with him. He furrowed his brow as he wrote notes in my chart, a look that seemed to imply he'd never before heard of the zaps. He looked up again.

"Are you exercising regularly?"

"No."

"How is your diet?"

"Gluttonous."

"Are you in therapy?"

"Yes."

After a brief lecture about the importance of diet, exercise, and what he called "healthy living," he grabbed a prescription pad and began to write on it with a purple plastic Ambien pen.

"I'm going to switch you to a new med-eee-cay-shun," he said. "Perhaps this will do a better job of treating your seem-tomes."

Perhaps? Don't you have anything stronger than "perhaps," Doc? Like "definitely"? This utter lack of accountability is one of the most frustrating parts of living with a mental illness. When you weed through the fancy terms and standard psychiatry boilerplate, you learn the entire class of these medications is virtually the same. The simple fact is that psychiatrists must play a trial-and-error game with each patient's brain chemistry until they find a pharmaceutical that works. The (educated) guessing game would have been acceptable if I was suffering from a hangnail or athlete's foot, but given that these "hope for the best" experiments directly affected my brain, and therefore my entire life, I was afraid. What if this pill makes me suicidal? Violent? Psychotic? Will my family be safe from me? Will I be able to work? These may sound like irrational and unrealistic manifestations of an imagination under the influence of rogue serotonin, but they were real to me. I didn't fully comprehend the fragility and fallibility of my brain until it broke down. And just as I do when a car or a computer is on the fritz, I wanted a professional to tell me exactly what was wrong and exactly how it could be fixed. But what I heard were vagaries and hypotheses about my brain, and rational or not, that's frightening.

Depression and anxiety are like this (I'm crossing my fingers). You rarely find one without the other, and that is both a blessing and a curse. Imagine yourself at a professional wrestling match, complete with the rabid, bloodthirsty fans and the over-the-top showmanship of the grapplers themselves. Suddenly, the lights go down and a white-hot spotlight signals the arrival of the meanest, dirtiest, scariest tag team around—the Comorbid Crushers. Two scoundrels, one named Depression and the other named Anxiety, both wearing black leather and the bone-chilling look of bloodlust. As they menacingly march toward the ring amid the deafening death metal and bright flashes of firepots, two security guards pull you from the crowd and throw you through the ropes. You are tonight's victim. *What?! No! I didn't sign up for this! I'm just a spectator!* Before you can stand or get your bearings, Depression launches himself from the top rope and drives his elbow right into your throat. You're down, disoriented, shocked. You reach for the bottom rope, hoping for leverage or escape, but before you can grip it—*BOOM!*—with another thunderous and excruciating thud, Anxiety piles on top of Depression. It's dark. You're numb, paralyzed, beaten. You're certain that the violence has broken something inside of you, but you don't know what or where. You consider fighting back, but why? With no strength, no leverage, no light, wouldn't it just be easier to lie there and die?

THIRTEEN

The gym I joined was called LA Fitness, which struck me as odd for a gym built in Orange County. If you've never lived in Southern California there's no way you can know that the people who live in the OC think the Los Angelinos who live forty minutes to our north are pretentious Hollywood scumbags with chronic road rage and a psychotic need to know exactly how many degrees of separation there are between themselves and Kevin Bacon. Conversely, residents of L.A. think those of us who live behind the Orange Curtain are surgically enhanced, spray-on tanned narcissists who wear acrylic heels to funerals and summon the day spa's receptionist to fetch us soy wheatgrass macchiatos while we're having our assholes bleached. I considered this conflict when I sat down to sign the contract that betrothed my frail frame to LA Fitness, but the peer pressure was just too relentless to let me back out.

Peer pressure. Yes. That's definitely the right term. See, when you become depressed, everyone you have ever known spontaneously becomes both an expert on mental illness and a habitual messenger of unsolicited advice. Many of these folks, while meaning well, are dumbshits. "Smoke some weed." "Jerk off more." "Come with me on this retreat to the desert where we bang on drums and wear Timberland gear and form a circle of trust where dudes can openly weep like little girls with skinned knees." Unfortunately, I also happen to have a circle of friends who *do* know what they're talking about when it comes to mental illness—and every one of them told me that regular exercise is *mandatory* for anyone with a depressive condition. I was advised by my therapist; my psychiatrist; my wife; my friend Dave (a therapist); his wife, Heather (a therapist); Dave's brother Kevin (a therapist); my friend Matt; his wife, Anat (educated as a therapist); and countless others that I should start exercising regularly.

Big problem.

I'm not particularly fond of exercise because I look like a total douche when I do it (Sharon: "You know what, Danny? You have a funny run. It looks . . . uncoordinated"), and if I'm being completely honest, my athletic resume is rather depressing. To wit:

1978: Played fullback (which is where coaches stick all of the "uncoordinated" kids because it's where they can do the least damage—as in, "Just stand there, Danny, and *whatever* you do, *do not kick the ball into our own goal again!*") for a Simi Valley Youth Soccer team called the Eager Beavers. We wore green shirts. I was number seven. A pair of women coached the team, and it took me twenty years to realize they were lesbian lovers and the name of the team was derived from their common enthusiasm for each other's genitalia. How awesome is *that*?

1985: Tried out for the Simi Valley High School freshman basketball team despite never having played even two seconds of organized hoop and not knowing the difference between zone defense and man-to-man defense. I've never admitted this to anyone but I temporarily lost control of my extremities in the first half hour of tryouts while running "suicides" during conditioning drills. Realized there's a reason why there aren't many Jewish dudes in the NBA; we suck. Quit tryouts after two days.

1992: Started at "left bench" for Fresno State University intramural basketball championship team. Took one shot all season. Airball. Remembered by teammates as a defensive stalwart because I once blocked a pass with my face.

1999: Accepted an invitation to play on a coed softball team with some coworkers. Went to Big 5 Sporting Goods store and purchased a full softball wardrobe (because there are two kinds of athletes: those who can play the game and those who camouflage their ghastly ineptitude with clothes that make them appear more fly), including something called "sliding pants." These are tight boxer briefs with extra padding on the outer thighs and butt cheeks, designed to protect one's caboose in the event that he has to slide into second base (which assumes that he somehow made it to first base—by no means a guarantee in my case). Struck out on first at-bat of the season (it should be noted that striking out in slow-pitch softball is quite difficult), quit the team due to unmitigated embarrassment in front of my coworkers, but kept the sliding pants because they make me look like I had a smattering of junk in my pathetic little trunk.

No matter how good I have *wanted* to be, or how good I have *tried* to be, I have never been a good athlete. More to the point, I've been a disgrace to competitive sport. So when everyone in my life told me I needed to exercise for the sake of my mental health, I resisted and ignored and tried everything I could to avoid it. The only thing that changed my mind was the depression itself, which pounded on my brain from the inside with such ferocity that I would have run through Times Square wearing nothing but sliding pants and pasties in the dead of winter if I thought it would help me feel better.

Despite my pattern of dismal failure in the domain of physical fitness, I'm fortunate enough to have married someone who could kick your ass without putting down her low-fat, hummus-filled, green tea pita. I decided to ask her for help with a new workout plan design because when it comes right down to it, I have no idea whatsoever what "working out" is supposed to look like. Sharon first suggested that any effective workout regimen should include a healthy dose of stretching. Given that there's only one muscle on my body that gets stretched with any regularity, I asked her to show me what she was talking about—and that may turn out to be the biggest mistake I've ever made. We sat side by side on the living room floor with our legs straight out in front of us. She told me to keep my back straight, reach forward with my arms, and touch my toes. *Ha! Aha! Aha-ha-ha-ha-haaaaa!* When my reach extended to the tops of my kneecaps, my hamstrings felt as though they'd been set alight. And then this woman, this masochist, this dealer of death that I married stood up, walked behind me, and put her hand on my back. Ever so gently, she pushed me farther forward—not far but certainly far enough to unleash muscular Armageddon upon the backs of my legs.

"Owwwww! Cut it out!"

"Quit crying, ya big baby," she said.

When I regained the ability to stand, Sharon continued to instruct me on the various ways one can contort his body in order to stretch various muscles and, as an added bonus, look like an idiot. It hurt. All of it. She told me stretching is a great way to squeeze the toxins out of my muscles, but if this excruciating pain was what it meant to be fit, I'd frankly prefer to be toxic.

A moment later we were standing, one foot in front

of ourselves, heel flexed, the other foot underneath us for support. Another hamstring stretch. As I tried not to fall down, I became aware that my right quad was shaking—and I'm not talking about normal, shiverlike shaking. It appeared as though someone was having a grand mal seizure in there. My muscle fibers quivered and trembled like swells on the ocean.

"Can you see that?" I asked.

"Yeah," she said. "That's not normal."

"What's that supposed to mean?"

"It means normal people's muscles don't shake like that," she said. "Your body is really, really weak. We have a lot of work to do."

"You go to hell, woman."

Sharon and I can do a lot of fun things together but exercising is not one of them. The sad side effect of her superior fitness is that she takes on this condescending attitude, as if she's one of those sadistic, butt-faced personal trainers from *The Biggest Loser* and her job is to scream *"Do it again, you pussy!"* until I puke or cry or suffer a prolapsed rectum. I needed to find something I could do *without* her—something she either could not or did not want to do—and the easy answer was basketball. She's five feet two and she shoots like a drunkard. I'm six feet three and I shoot like an Eager Beaver. I may have a funny run, but you can't teach tall, baby. It was time for me to get my Mike Smrek* on, and I joined LA Fitness because it had a

* A stiff, "gangly," Canadian, seven-foot white guy (and by

basketball court in the very back section of the gym, far from the potentially disapproving and horrified gazes of the armchair Marv Alberts riding those high-stepping elliptical trainer machines that make people look like they're trying to get their thong underwear out of their butts without using their hands.

All you really need to know about my return to the court is this: before the end of my first game, I was outside lying prostrate on the ground and gasping for breath. I stayed in that position until one of my team-mates walked over and said, "Are you dying?"

"Depends," I said. "Are we winning?"

It was so much worse than I'd expected. I was a di-saster. My legs felt like quivering gravy, my back ached from shoulders to ass crack, and my pride needed defi-brillation urgently. As it turns out, a return to physical activity after a long respite should be progressive. Start with shorter workouts and work your way up until your lungs remember what it means to breathe. Con-versely, storming back with a full-court basketball game in a hot, poorly ventilated gym does to one's lungs what a burning cigarette butt does to a hillside covered with dry brush. Beyond merely losing any semblance of cardiovascular stamina since I'd last played, my "feel" for the game had vanished entirely. I was a fish out of water before the game was three min-

---

"white" I mean "practically translucent") who backed up Ka-reem Abdul-Jabbar when the Lakers won back-to-back NBA championships in 1986–87.

utes old, running around the court like a blind man, forcing ridiculous passes into infinitesimal spots, and permitting the man I was supposed to defend to saunter right up to the basket for an easy layup. Still, my teammates saw fit to pass me the ball, perhaps out of pity. I hit two three-pointers and grabbed a few rebounds, but I also hit the side of the backboard twice, which is basketball's equivalent of shitting the bed.

I had become a typical, slovenly American male. Were it not for my genetic predisposition to thinness, I'd be a six-hundred-pound, mouth-breathing lummox who sits on the couch and spends his days checking his belly rolls for errant snack cakes. Guys my age should have long since surrendered to the laws of whatever it is that cripples people who try to exert themselves beyond the boundaries of common sense. When I was a younger basketball player, I thought the guys my age were pathetic. They didn't belong on the court. They were the codgers whose oncoming dementia made them pass the ball to the wrong team and whose Achilles tendons would rip like a paper towel from a perforated roll of Brawny and curl up into their calves like a window shade. I had become that guy. Pass the BENGAY.

I would have found a way to persevere if the exercise made me feel the way everyone said it would. If I had been exhilarated and reenergized, if I felt more alive, if I felt I was giving my brain the endorphins it needed to heal itself, I would have continued to fight through the abuse the workouts wrought upon my pride and my body. But I never got there. I never felt as though my overall mood was influenced in either direction by the effort, and I quit going to the gym. On the positive side, I saved my $35-per-month membership fee (which, for the record, I did not use to pay for asshole bleaching).

FOURTEEN

I hated my sister on Tuesday nights. I hated her because she was the only person standing between the Fonz and me.

"Happy Days," I pleaded.

"No," Debbie said. *"Little House on the Prairie."*

"We watched that *last* week."

"So . . . ?"

"So . . . kiss my butt."

"Mom!" she shouted.

My mother was Deb's closer when it came to *Little House*, but to her it was more an issue of civic pride than entertainment value, or (as was the case for my sister) a crush on the Ingallses' adopted little brother, Albert. *Little House on the Prairie* was filmed in the hills north of Simi Valley, and because my parents moved to Simi from Encino in 1972, my mom was a cheerleader for all things Simi. The chance to see the outer limits of our town on television every Tuesday was too thrilling to pass up, even if it meant enduring my whining about not getting to see Carmine "the Big Ragu" from *Laverne & Shirley* guest star next to Fonzie that night.

I wanted to despise *Little House*, but over time I was forced to watch it so frequently that I developed crushes on both Laura and Mary Ingalls, and a deep, visceral hatred for that crazy, conniving bitch, Nellie Oleson. I had a recurring dream of her being run over by a rickety covered wagon driven by one of the snake-oil salesmen who rolled into town to hock his miracle hair tonics and virility potions. It's ironic that I abhorred her so lustfully, because all these years later, crazy Nellie is the character I relate to the most. Well, she and the snake-oil salesman.

It's easy to believe antidepressants are snake oil, too. The way they're marketed to consumers—"You're sad now, but take this and you'll be happy, happy, happy!"—does little to offer any sort of clinical legitimacy. The consumer-directed commercials for these meds strike me as modernized, higher-production-value regurgitations of what street dealers might say when trying to sell ecstasy or meth to some Wall Street moron: "I've got some shit that will take you to the ultimate happy place, bro. First one's free, but I'll be here if you need another hit." What sucks is in this present-day dealer scenario, the customer has almost no choice but to take the pill; he's in no position to take the higher moral ground. At least *I* wasn't. Given the desperation and aimlessness I was experiencing, I would have believed in almost anything that came with the promise of making me feel better. Snake oil, Zoloft, ecstasy . . . what's the difference when you're depressed? Just give me something. *Anything!*

I ended up with Zoloft for no reason other than that was what was given to me. I would like to be able to brag about what a smart consumer I was when it came to drugs designed to alter my brain chemistry, but I was no such thing. This decision wasn't like buying a new mattress or a minivan or a good winter coat; this was me merely trying to stay alive and sane. I therefore did not consult *Consumer Reports*. I did not ask for references or clinical trial findings or even for a second opinion. I took the doctor's word for it, took the prescription, and took the pill. I believed it would work because it just had to, and ultimately it did. I consider myself fortunate that I found relief from my first antidepressant prescription because I just as easily could have ended up like the girl in the opening credits of *Little House on the Prairie*, who, while running with her sisters down a hillside flecked with knee-high grasses, trips over her own feet and does a face-plant right into the north end of Simi Valley.

But after a little over a year on the same prescription, I felt a precipitous drop in the efficacy of my Zoloft.

It was not as though I fell back to rock bottom, but the symptoms that had been masked or diminished by the medication seemed to creep back. It was quite subtle at first. Hardly noticeable really. But the fatigue and dizziness became more severe every few days or so, and I was not about to be patient with it.

"Good afternoon," Emily answered. "Dr. Nima's office."

"Uh, hi, uh, Emily. My name is Daniel Evans. I'm a patient of Dr. Nima's?"

"Yes, hi, Danny. I remember you."

(Oh my Gee-Dash-Dee. She remembers me. Not sure if that's good or bad, but let's go with good.)

"Hi. Um, I was wondering if Dr. Nima has any availability this afternoon. I think I might need to have my meds adjusted."

I heard the sound of pages turning on the other end of the line. "It looks like we have four forty-five available. Will that work for you?"

"Perfect. Thank you so much, Emily."

"Uh-huh." Click.

I began to second-guess myself immediately. Was I over the top? I've had a habit all my life of being too grateful for things, so much so that I come off fake and weird. Maybe the "so much" wasn't necessary. Shit. Now it was going to be awkward when I got to Dr. Nima's office. Emily would look at my eyes, trying to read them, which would make it virtually impossible to stare at her boobs because she'd see me doing so, snap her fingers at me and say, "Hey! Eyes up here, pal." Then I'd have to make some sort of threatening move so as to make her fear for her life, which would then motivate her to let me stare directly at her breasts, which was scientifically proven to calm the savage beast whose Zoloft is taking a dump. I'm really not good with threatening moves. I don't like confrontation.

When I got to the office, Emily smiled. Then she looked down and continued to fill out some insurance form. I stared right at her breasts for a really long time. No faux attempted murder necessary.

Dr. Nima called me in, sat me down, asked me if I had thoughts about killing myself or anyone else (to which I responded in the negative), and then asked me to describe what was happening. I recounted the subtle, steady upswing in my symptoms.

"I'm fatigued more often than I was when the Zoloft was working well," I said. "Those zaps have returned, too. And I guess the most disturbing part is that I've started to get that melancholy mood far too often for my comfort."

"Yes," he said, "I think I can tell you what is happening. There is a fee-nom-ee-non called Prozac Poop-Out. Have you ever heard of this fee-nom-ee-non?"

Blink. Blink blink.

"You see, Mr. Eee-vans, every human body is different. Sometimes a med-ee-cay-shun will work very well for one man for many, many, many years, but for another man it is not quite right. Your body appears to fall somewhere in between, meaning the med-ee-cay-shun worked well for you for some time, but now your body has developed a tolerance to it. Your body is stronger than the med-ee-cay-shun."

"Awesome," I said. "Does this mean I'm resistant to antidepressants?"

"Not ness-ee-saree-lee. It simply means that we must begin to try other SSRIs until we find one that works."

"Okay."

"Now . . . are there any med-ee-cay-shuns that you would like to try first?"

"What? No. You're my doctor so I'll take your advice. What do *you* think?"

"Well, I would like to start you on lakes-uh-pro," he said.

"Lexapro?"

"Yes. Lakes-uh-pro. This is a very good med-ee-cay-shun, also an SSRI, but slightly different kem-ee-call compo-zee-shun than Zoloft."

It's striking how easily I was convinced to try different antidepressant meds. Even buying something as simple as barbecue sauce would have required more study and consideration than this. But I was completely in the dark, completely at the whim of my psychiatrist, and no amount of study or research in *Consumer Reports* would better inform me because, as the man said, every man is different. Every brain is different.

Every med-ee-cay-shun is different. It's trial and error. Fortunately, both Lexapro and Zoloft are classified as SSRIs, which meant I didn't have to wean myself from one before starting the other. It did not, however, mean that I could reclaim full working control of my penis.

FIFTEEN

I parked my car facing the street and watched through my rearview mirror as the others arrived. Many of them were talking on cell phones as they pulled into the parking lot, some hurriedly trying to end their conversations so they could get out of their cars and renew acquaintances with their friends. They all seemed to know each other. I spied on them milling about, telling jokes, hugging as they walked toward the church, and I felt my palms begin to sweat, my heart rate jump. I didn't want to go in. More specifically, I didn't want to have to face what I thought I might find inside. But I was fully aware that my desire to sidestep (if not ignore altogether) potentially ugly truths was what had brought me to that freshly paved church parking lot in the first place, and that's why I went in.

In a moment of paralyzing emotional sobriety, I allowed myself to consider the possibility that I had a drinking problem. Whether that was a function of Sharon's indefatigable denunciation of my consumption or my own fear about how right she may have been, it was clear that I had lost all objectivity on the matter and my uncertainty about it was frightening. She and I each held our own strong biases about the appropriateness (or lack thereof) of my drinking, and I suddenly felt a panic about it. I needed to know which of us was right. I went online to find an Alcoholics Anonymous meeting without telling Sharon I was going to do so. Two hours later, with my resolve shivering like a wet dog, I walked in.

The room was long and narrow, carpeted with the dense, gray, industrial weave you often see in office suites, government buildings, and houses of worship like the one I'd come to. This was my first foray into a megachurch, as they were dubbed by the mildly creative news media when they investigated the alleged moral and ethical foibles of televangelists like Jim Bakker, Jimmy Swaggart, and Jerry Falwell. Dozens of glossy gray metal chairs were scattered throughout the megameeting room, but the other attendees seemed to know instinctively that the chairs should be arranged in rows and facing the long wooden table against the seemingly endless wall that stretched out past the door. I took a seat in the back, on the end, and listened to the people talk about their job frustrations, their hunger, and their gratitude that they were able to come to this meeting. I felt disastrously out of place. I felt embarrassed. But I had to be sure that I truly didn't belong there.

A man with lots of sloppy tattoos on his arms came into the room. He made a C with his thumb and index finger, stuck it in his mouth, and produced a loud, high-pitched whistle. I've always wanted to be able to do that.

"Everyone grab a seat!" he bellowed. "We're going to get started."

Although I can vividly remember the efficiency of his words and the orderly, controlled cadence with which he spoke, the content of his speech has left me. I was too busy judging. It was my first AA meeting, my first time sitting among a demographic about which I knew only one thing: I desperately wanted *not* to belong to it. They were drunks. Addicts. The dregs of society. These were broken people, and while I had long since come to the realization that I too was broken, I tried strenuously for many weeks to convince myself that I was not quite *this* broken—that I was not an alcoholic. In the early stages of my depression, when my subconscious mind preyed on my own spectacular gullibility and machismo, I could easily have persuaded myself to believe I was better than these folks. But now I knew better than to trust my own self-perception. Though it was more difficult, more embarrassing, more likely to expose me to something I would prefer not to know about myself, I knew I needed to be in *that* church, at *that* time, with *those* people. I needed to know.

A man in the second row stood.

"Jake. Alcoholic."

"Hi, Jake," everyone said in unison.

Jake announced that he was celebrating his seventh month of sobriety—a revelation that drew light applause and cheers from the other attendees—but his demeanor struck me. He was not making a victory speech, not boasting that he had slain the dragon. Despite his accomplishment, he still wore the face of spiritual exhaustion and spoke with the tenor of a beaten man. Other people stood and spoke during the hour, some sharing tales about how they'd been in situations that put temptation within reach. Many talked about the "steps" and the importance of the people in the room in saving their lives. Some were handed metal pieces of varying sizes and colors, the larger coins reserved for those who had gone the longest without a drink.

I made the assessment early in the meeting that I wasn't an alcoholic. Although I had consumed more than my fair share of beer in the previous months, the drive to drink was a want, not an unrelenting physical need. I did not have a problem going days or weeks without alcohol—I just chose not to take such extended leaves of absence from it. The descriptions by others of their blackouts, their homelessness, their severe health problems were unfamiliar to me, and I took it as a fairly clear signal that I was not an addict. But that didn't mean I didn't belong in that room. When I cast the drinking part of the equation aside, it occurred to me that I wasn't that much different than the others in that meeting. In fact, we were very much alike.

I couldn't stop thinking about Jake. Whenever another speaker said something emotional or profound, I looked back at Jake to gauge his reaction. I wanted to be inside his head. I wanted to know how it felt to have rescued one's self from destitution without any sense of accomplishment or safety. How did it feel to rely so heavily on the support of others? The more I contemplated it, the more it became clear that I knew exactly how those things felt. I had lived them myself. I, too, had stuffed undesirable feelings deep down inside myself and buried them under vices. I, too, needed to know that there were others out there feeling the way I did. I, too, needed to know I was supported in deed, not just in word.

When the meeting adjourned, I left hastily. I was scared. And I wanted to get out of there before I saw or heard something that might have changed my own self-assessment.

SIXTEEN

The immense Zenith television in the middle of the living room of my childhood home was nothing spectacular in terms of size or color or definition; it was the rotund electrical gut behind the tube that gave the TV its tremendous girth and weight. My father used to tell Debbie and me not to sit too close to the TV, not because he thought it would ruin our eyes but because we lived in earthquake-prone Southern California. The Zenith weighed upwards of 150 pounds and my dad didn't want us to get crushed under the flickering image of H.R. Pufnstuf.

Through that TV screen I began to understand human emotion. I cried when it showed the Celtics beating my beloved Lakers in the NBA finals. I discovered the essence of coolness when my hero, the Fonz, jumped over a row of garbage cans on his motorcycle and then stuck his tongue down Pinky Tuscadero's throat. And the night my parents finally acquired one of the pirated cable boxes about which their Temple Jewey Jew-Jew friends spoke so effusively, I snuck into the living room at two in the morning and saw, for the first time in my life, a topless woman. My sock drawer hasn't been the same since.

Technology being what it was in the late '70s and early '80s, our big old Zenith had a tendency to deliver humor to our living room in ways other than Boss Hogg's frustration at failing to "git them Duke boys." When the networks had a problem relaying their programming to the living rooms of America, they broadcast a static blue screen with the words PLEASE STAND BY in big, bold, white text. Whenever that occurred, it was a family tradition for us all to stand up, walk over to the TV set, and "stand by" it until the show came back on.

But by far the best entertainment we ever got from that Zenith occurred when it broke down. My dad was a mechanical engineer. In his spare time he derived great pleasure from taking random problems from Debbie's trigonometry and calculus textbooks and solving them. That was his idea of fun; it was my idea of finishing dead last in the game of genetic roulette. But despite his penchant for understanding complex concepts and fixing difficult problems, a busted TV set was his kryptonite. When the picture got fuzzy or the vertical hold went haywire on us, he'd turn beet red, and I soon learned that was my cue to leave the room.

I lived in fear of my father's moods because our home environment was inexorably linked to his personal levels of anger and frustration. This is not to say that every moment of my childhood was fraught with unease and resignation. It most certainly wasn't. Mine is not a tale of child abuse or of alcoholic parents. I'm grateful that I was raised in a home by parents who never divorced. They loved us and we knew it, and I've seen enough to know that those simple things are not so simple. My dad was capable of great joy, and some of my fondest memories are the times when he would laugh so hard that the only sound he could produce was a faint, high-pitched wail. But those moments were intertwined with resounding expressions of irascibility.

One night he came home from work in a volatile mood, and his attitude deteriorated further when he and my mother engaged in an argument about something. By the time we all sat down at the dining room table to eat, he was practically seething. I distinctly remember trying to avoid his gaze, instead directing every ounce of my attention to the task of spinning my fork around in the center of my plate in an attempt to trap as much spaghetti and meat sauce as possible. As I twirled my flatware, my mom said something that put my dad over the top. He picked up his loaded plate with one hand and hurled it against the wall. He shouted as he did so, and then he stormed out of the room. I can still remember the rage on his face.

For a split second there was silence. Shock.

The white ceramic plate sat in shards at the base of the wall, little chips of it mixed in with the pasta like big chunks of Parmesan. A broad stroke of deep red Ragu pocked with tiny pieces of ground meat shrapnel blanketed the white wall, its streaks representative of a slow, suicidal slide down to the pale blue carpet. (I heard once that the best way to see if pasta was properly cooked was to throw it at the wall and see if it sticks, but it was clear that my dad had followed that rule with a bit too much gusto.)

Debbie cried first. Our dad was a giant to us: six feet four, strong build, strong spirit. The sight of a man that big throwing a plate that full at a wall that close was extraordinarily frightening to us. But since I was the Peacemaker in our home, the one who made it his job to keep everyone happy happy happy, my eyes stayed focused on my mother. I would take my cue to cry or not based on her reaction to the cacophony. She sat stoically, but when I saw a single tear break free from her lower lid and plummet down her right cheek, I knew it was okay to let go.

This sort of outburst didn't happen every day, but it was frequent enough that (as a defense mechanism) Debbie and I started to find humor in our dad's anger, especially when it was directed at others.

Although he had no formal training or education,

my dad was something of an honorary rabbi in our community. Most nights, after dinner, he would retreat to my parents' bedroom, close the door, and study his Torah, Talmud, and Hebrew texts until Debbie and I went in to kiss him good night. He was active in our synagogue, and almost by default he became the "rabbi" to whom many Jewish parents brought their children when the time came to prepare for a Bar/Bat Mitzvah. A rite of passage for thirteen-year-old Jewish kids, this event is considered the moment when the child becomes an adult in the eyes of Gee-Dash-Dee. It's a big deal for the Jews, more meaningful maybe than the child's first time getting "accidentally" blitzed on Manischewitz wine (*cough* Debbie! *cough*), so the moms and dads make a big production out of it. Several nights a week, kids would come to our house and more or less perform for my dad—in Hebrew—and Gee-Dash-Dee help them if they came unprepared.

Since watching TV in the living room would have been a distraction to the victim, the three of us—my sister, my mother, and I—huddled in my parents' bedroom to watch *Wheel of Fortune.* But we always kept the door open just enough so we could hear what was happening out there, and because many of the students were our friends and/or Hebrew school classmates, we had a strong handle on who would do well and who would incur my dad's wrath. We never kept statistics on such things, but I'd estimate about 35 percent of the kids left our house in tears. Debbie and I loved that because, well, we were just glad it wasn't us.

———

I have never been in a fight. Not a fistfight, not a heated political argument, not a debate where voices and/or ire are raised—nothing of the sort. If I'm dining in a restaurant and my food is served cold or gross or just wrong, I find it easier to eat it than to send it back and risk agitating the chef or waiter. There are a scant few causes or ideals about which I feel especially passionate or rigid, and I believe this is inexorably linked to my fear of confrontation; if I don't care enough about something, I won't be compelled to stick up for it when push literally and figuratively comes to shove. The Beastie Boys demanded in the 1980s that I had to fight for my right to party—and it's hard for me to take issue with the greatest triumvirate of Jewish guys this side of Genesis (the book in the Bible, not Phil Collins's band)—but if that were indeed the case I probably would have avoided any such fisticuffs and just gone home to watch *SportsCenter*.

"Intellectually, I know why I'm like this," I told Susan. "I remember how scared I was of my dad's temper."

"Did you think he was going to hurt you?" she asked.

"No. I knew he wouldn't. He was not physically violent with any of us."

"Then what was it? What about his temper was so frightening to you?"

I stared out the window to my left, through the

dusty white slats on the mini-blinds and into the reflective windows of the small office building across the street. When the sun was setting, its glare bounced right off of those windows and into Susan's office with such a blinding glare that she had to close the blinds. But with sunset still a few hours away, I had a clear view of the building and its gaudy, silver Coastal County Loan and Title sign.

"I think a lot of it was his size," I guessed aloud.

"How do you mean?"

"I mean that I was just a little kid, you know? And here was this tall, loud, intimidating man yelling and throwing plates at the wall and nearly losing control of himself. It freaked me out."

"I'm sure it did," Susan said. "Did you always know where his anger was coming from?"

"Well, that's a hard one to answer because, I mean, yes, there was always some sort of a catalyst, some argument with my mom or experience at work that pissed him off. There was always a spark. But as I've grown older and more aware, it's become clear to me that there was a chronic readiness in him to explode. Do you know what I mean? It's like he was built of tinder straw and brush, and just that one little spark was all it took to set him off."

"And you have no idea why he was predisposed to such anger?" she asked.

"No," I said, "but I'd sure like to find out."

SEVENTEEN

Were it not for my unchecked disdain for almost everything about Judaism, I would have been a kick-ass rabbi. That was the career path onto which my parents delivered me before my earliest memory. I believed they were serious about my future in the rabbinical arts, and not just because three evenings each week, while other boys my age were at baseball practice, my scrawny ass was sitting in a classroom at our synagogue. I could write my name in Hebrew but I knew nothing about turning a double play. I could recite the prayers one must chant before reading from the Torah, but I had no idea why ballplayers put black makeup under their eyes. And that's only scratching the surface of the social consequences a Jewboy confronts.

We've all heard myriad horror stories about the rigors and disciplinarian environment of Catholic school, but some of those tales sound like a bowl of Lucky Charms when contrasted against Hebrew school. Anyone who has seen five minutes of a Woody Allen film knows Jewish discipline and control are grounded in the impenetrable bedrock of guilt. If you think corporal punishment applied by Sister Mary is rough, try telling Mrs. Mendelbaum, a Jewish widow, that Jews should be allowed to eat bacon because it tastes so good. In a matter of forty-five seconds, she can make a boy believe such a heinously goyish attitude is a clear indication that his entire life is an abomination and the only way to save himself from Gee-Dash-Dee's wrath is to come to her house and mow the lawn her dear departed Mordechai, *alav ha-shalom*, may Gee-Dash-Dee rest his soul, used to mow on Tuesday mornings in nothing but a white undershirt, boxer shorts, and sandals with black socks.

The only thing I liked about Hebrew school was the occasional opportunity to discuss the small army of Jews who played in the major leagues. Throughout the decades many Jewish ballplayers reached Hall of Fame status—Hank Greenberg, Sandy Koufax, even Rod Carew.* Everything else about Hebrew school sucked.

---

* Carew is not known to have formally converted to Judaism, but he married a Jewish woman and appeared on the cover of the July 18, 1977, issue of *Time* magazine wearing a "Chai" necklace.

I hated being there. I longed to be outside fielding grounders or catching pop flies, not sulking in a synagogue.

"*Ah-nee ro-tzeh bay-gel*, Mrs. Mendelbaum."

I said it dutifully every time, even when I wanted to say, "Just give me the damn bagel, Mendelbitch."

Judaism was thrust upon me so relentlessly—Hebrew school, Friday night services, Saturday morning services, Shabbat dinners, Bar Mitzvah training, a class on how to sing Torah scriptures based on lines and squiggles called *trope*—that I wanted almost nothing to do with it. But that wasn't my choice to make. My father decided I was going to be a great Jewish scholar and no further discussion was necessary. There was discipline if I resisted and praise when I complied. I wanted the praise. I needed it. Since I had so little control over my own choices, my only gauge of the kind of person I was becoming was external—my dad. My happiness was not particularly relevant unless he was happy with me, too, and that foundational confusion has stayed with me into my adult life. I seek approval from others, oftentimes in the form of humor, and my emotional resilience rises and falls with the effusiveness of these external validations. I have trouble determining my own self-worth.

There are a number of different sects within the Jewish community, but the three most prominent in my parents' conversations were Reform, Conservative, and Orthodox. Those who chose to align themselves with a Reform synagogue were still considered Jews, but just barely. They bucked the inalienable demands of Conservative Jews by ignoring Gee-Dash-Dee's commandments to wear a yarmulke and separate dairy products from meat (no cheeseburgers), and there was an evil but unconfirmed rumor that some of them even allowed women to become rabbis. *Gasp!* At the other end of the spectrum were the Orthodox Jews, who were all Jew, all the time, amen. They wore those curly sideburns (*payes*), walked to the synagogue on Shabbat, and had blessings for everything—including taking a dump! *Freaks!*

We belonged to a Conservative *shul*, which was the religious equivalent of medium-rare. We were serious, but not too serious, and you could still see a little pink in the center. It didn't feel medium to me, though; we may as well have been living on a kibbutz in Israel as far as I was concerned. Saturday morning services were two and a half hours of torture. Bow to the ark, pound your chest, close your eyes, talk to Gee-Dash-Dee, put on your *tallis*, kiss the fringes, stand up, sit down, *fight fight fight!* Though most of what was spoken aloud was Hebrew, I would follow along in the English translation and routinely find myself stupefied by the content. I didn't believe a word of it. On virtually every page of the prayer book, Gee-Dash-Dee was referenced as this King Kong–like holy giant who did all of this crazy, unbelievable stuff back in the day.

Hear O Israel! The Lord is Our Gee-Dash-Dee! The Lord is One! Blessed are You, O Lord, King of the Universe, Who hath brought our people out of Egypt. Who hath created a whale that swallowed Jonah whole and then barfed him out. Who hath created bushes that talk (think I saw that in a porno once) and rivers that turn to blood and fathers so overwhelmed by your nonsense that they'd actually consider killing their own sons.

Was I expected to believe this crap? Was this the kind of nonsense I was supposed to sling when I became a rabbi? No way. No *way*! I didn't believe a word of it, and I was shocked that my father—a mathematician who believed in the absoluteness of numbers and science and facts—actually gave this gibberish credence. But he was a Believer, and that wasn't going to change. If I wanted his approval (which I desperately did), I was going to have to play along despite my repulsion. True to my trademark overzealousness, I overshot the runway on my efforts to do so. I gave away too much of myself.

During my sophomore year in high school, I volunteered to my dad that I wanted to go to a Yeshiva—a Jewish high school where heavy emphasis is placed on learning Hebrew, studying the Torah, and further accelerating separation from the *goyish* norm. Obviously, I was lying. I couldn't think of anything I wanted less than to be surrounded by that bullshit and wear the scarlet Hebrew letter of "Yeshiva Boy." But if it meant making my dad proud of me, I'd do it. With twenty years of hindsight, I now look back on this proffer as a measure of my need for approval. I so sincerely wanted to please my dad that I considered doing something I absolutely despised, something that would have been absolute torture to me. To his credit, I think my dad knew I was full of it. I think he could see and hear that my heart really wasn't in it, and he talked me out of it. I don't have the words to thank him for that.

Before the first semester of my senior year at Simi Valley High School,* I had a list of classes I could take to earn some "elective" credits. I naturally sought out a class that could (a) be easy, (b) be passed with minimal effort, and (c) put me as close to cute girls as possible. I chose a gourmet cooking class based almost entirely on the assumption that the hot, public school cheerleaders and their soft, supple, almost fully developed breasts would be taking the class to learn how to cook for their jock boyfriends. *"Oops, you have some baking soda on the front of your Springsteen concert T-shirt, Ashley. Allow me to remove it for you. With my tongue!"*

Three weeks into the semester my dad caught wind that I was enrolled in a cooking class.

"Nice Jewish boys do not take cooking classes!" he barked, just before he ordered me to drop the class and

---

* Simi High's most famous alumnus, Don MacLean, graduated the same year I did and went on to make millions in the NBA. Ironically, I went on to a career in sports, as well; I fielded angry phone calls from the irate parents of Little Leaguers whom I'd failed to mention in my newspaper articles.

pick something more intellectual—something befitting the future figurehead of Simi Valley's humble Jewish community, where you could be part of the *minyan* as long as you had a circumcised penis, a big nose, or an affinity for Woody Allen movies. The only other elective option available to me was Basic Principles of Accounting, taught by Mrs. Anderson, who smelled like boiled cabbage.

With due respect to those of you who make your living with balance sheets and whatnot, it's my feeling that accounting sucks big, sweaty, wrinkled-up donkey balls covered in pickle juice. I don't know what kind of sadistic human being could possibly derive pleasure or fulfillment from such madness. For starters, accounting is largely about math, and to me that makes it a stain on humanity. I hate math. I hate it in the same purely visceral way people hate communism and e-mail spam and Simon Cowell. And because I hated it, I sucked at it. And given that I had to catch up on three weeks' worth of ledgers and profit/loss statements while simultaneously keeping pace with the rest of the class on the new material, I went teats-up in very short order. I failed the class.

(This just in: Nice Jewish Boys don't bring home Fs.)

I knew a serious smack-down was imminent so I conspired to get home from school as fast as possible each day and be the first one to the mailbox. More specifically, the first one to intercept my report card. Success! My parents continued to ask me if the report had arrived, and for three weeks I shrugged my shoulders and told them no, it hadn't. *"Must have gotten lost in the mail. Weird, huh?"*

It was a Sunday when they found out. Just as my sister and I were about to go to the movie theater to see *Little Shop of Horrors* for the third time, I was summoned to the living room by the voice I always feared as a kid. The voice of Your Father. It was deep and intense. Villainous. The moment I heard it, I knew I was completely hosed. (One of my favorite therapeutic discoveries was the revelation that my proximity to anger as a kid conditioned me to fear that behavior. As a result, situations and experiences that would trigger rage in others instead propelled me into depression. In short, if given a choice between anger and total numbness, my brain preferred to feel nothing at all.)

I was confronted. I admitted guilt. I was sent to my room to await sentencing, without so much as an "Officer Burrell has some documents for you to sign," which even the mouth-breathing morons on *The People's Court* were told after they'd been handed their asses by Judge Wapner.

It hadn't occurred to me that the most egregious of my crimes was neither the F nor the lying; it was robbing my father of his control. I took ownership of the situation (albeit temporarily) on my own and left my dad in the precarious posture of obliviousness. He felt victimized and disrespected.

A few days later, they sent me to see Neil Diamond. The therapist, not the real Neil. And you know how *that* turned out.

In therapy with Susan, the first scapegoat I identified as the root of my earthly misery was my career—rather, my lack thereof. I was thirty-two years old, and while my friends and peers were attorneys or VPs of sales or some other species of wealth-building big shot, where was I? Where was my wealth? Where was my security? For many men, self-worth is a mirrored reflection of net worth, and by that standard I wasn't worth much at all. That's what I believed. And that's how I felt. I felt like nothing.

"Why do you think you've had so much trouble finding a job that satisfies you?" Susan asked.

"I have dueling priorities. I'd obviously prefer to have a job that makes me feel good about myself. Who wouldn't? But I have a family to provide for now, and I've had to suspend my search for satisfaction because I have obligations. Money and benefits and health insurance are more important than my happiness right now."

"Do you think there's any way to have both income *and* satisfaction?"

"No," I said. "I couldn't expose Sharon and Noah to that kind of peril. It's my job to keep them safe."

"Safe?" she asked. "Tell me what you mean by that."

I once heard a therapist refer to meaningful, paradigm-shifting discoveries in counseling as "aha moments," and this was my first one. I had theretofore believed that safety and control were conjoined twins. A good job was a safe job: decent pay, good benefits, little exposure to risk. My obligation was not to be happy; it was to provide. Satisfaction was a nice concept, but not a priority. As long as my wife and child were cared for financially, all was well. Happiness would come from somewhere else. From Gee-Dash-Dee perhaps. Or from knowing I was protecting my family. Work and joy need not interfere with one another. Until Susan challenged me to define that safety, I never questioned it. To me, it was as True and Real as the blueness of the sky. But I saw the idiocy in that point of view the moment I heard her query, and I wanted to know why I'd believed in it for so long.

Susan and I pursued this path vigorously during our sessions, and beneath the layer of skin we peeled back was a clear picture of just how much my dad's fury and the constant control had blazed the trail upon which my life was based. There were moments during our conversations when I retreated to the darkest corners of my memory. I'd sit in silence, sometimes with my head in my hands, and when I reengaged my consciousness, I brought with me a certain anecdote or recollection. Although I didn't realize it at the time, each time I went into that place I returned with another piece of a giant puzzle, and over time the picture grew a little clearer.

I wanted as a kid to play Little League baseball. I can vividly recall closing my eyes and imagining myself wearing the funny stirrup socks and a uniform with EVANS printed across my shoulder blades in iron-on black letters. I would wear the same number 15 that my favorite player, Davey Lopes, wore on the back of his Los Angeles Dodgers uniform. Yet each time I raised the idea of signing up for Little League, I was reminded that such a commitment would interfere with my religious education. I temporarily relented each time I was shot down, but sooner or later I repeated my request.

My mother came to me with a newspaper clipping when I was eleven years old. " 'Pitch, Hit and Run' competition this weekend at Rancho Simi Community Park. All ages."

"Would you like to go?" she asked me.

"Are you serious?" I bellowed. "Yes! Yes, yes, yes!" I couldn't believe I'd finally broken through to them.

(It should be noted that I'd never really competed for anything as an individual. I played soccer, a *team* sport, but the concept of being thrust into an every-man-for-himself challenge was entirely foreign to me. I was oblivious.)

I arrived at the park dressed in the most athletically appropriate clothing I could find in my dresser: Puma tennis shoes, ankle-high white tube socks, shorts, and my Dodgers T-shirt. But as soon as I walked inside the chain-link-walled dugout, it was clear that I wasn't like the other boys who'd signed up. Everyone else was wearing a Little League uniform, including the funny stirrup socks and jerseys with their last names printed across the shoulder blades in iron-on black letters. I recognized some of the boys from school, most notably Scott and Stuart Bradshaw. They were twins but Scott was noticeably larger than Stuart, and everyone in school who had seen him play believed he would end up in the major leagues someday.

I don't need to tell you how the competition went; I was a disaster. I swung and missed at every pitch while others hit stinging line drives and deep fly balls. When our speed running around the bases was timed, those with proper cleats flew through the diamond, while I slipped and sputtered on the reddish-brown infield dirt. None of my pitches even made it to home plate. The other boys tried to hide their ridicule at first but I made it harder for them with each subsequent challenge.

That was my first and last experience with Little League baseball.

"I was humiliated," I told Susan, my eyes pointed at the carpet. "I never again asked my parents to sign me up for baseball."

Susan knew where I was going with this. She didn't try to stop me.

"In the long run I guess my dad got what he wanted. Baseball no longer distracted me from my religious studies. I don't think he and my mom intended for the competition to go the way it did; they couldn't have known how bad I was or how good the other boys were. But it's hard for me to look back on that day and *not* feel like I was manipulated and controlled in some way. It was as if they were saying, you know, 'You wanted to play baseball, so here: go play some baseball. But don't come crying to us when it doesn't work out because, after all, we were the people who told you to focus on Hebrew school.' "

I stopped talking for a moment while my mind feverishly processed the greater meaning of what I'd just recalled. To me, this is the very best part of therapy—the silent, intensely contemplative moments when the clouds part and I finally understand an important part of myself or my life for the first time.

"I feel like I never learned how to compete, and that has cost me some important opportunities in life," I said. "My life has been all about taking what's given to me. Get whatever job you can get instead of going after what I really want. Take what is safe and certain. Settle. Don't make waves. That's what I took away from Hebrew education. *This is what God said and it's not going to change so just do and believe what He tells you to do.* There are no life lessons in that for me. What would really have come in handy for me is an education in how to decide and go after what *I* wanted, not what *someone else* wanted for me on my behalf. *That's* the kind of control I'm talking about."

"Do you still feel like you're being controlled by someone else?" Susan asked.

"No. I feel like my life is *out* of control right now. That's why I'm here. I need help putting a tent over the circus my life has become."

EIGHTEEN

I cracked a lot of jokes in therapy, just as I did in conversations with the other people in my life. For our first few sessions, Susan was a perfect audience. She laughed genuinely and heartily at the silly things I'd say in the midst of this outpouring or that. I never got the idea that she was merely indulging me, and I don't believe she was, but there came a point when her reactions to my jokes became more subdued. There were uncomfortable silences after my witty comments. I found them disarming. Painful.

I've always been the funny guy, and while there have been hundreds of times when the ability to make people laugh or lighten up has been a blessing, there also have been moments in my life—particularly during my adolescence and early adulthood—when my instinct and reflexive need to be witty have deepened my sorrow and exposed my fragile ego to crushing blows of rejection.

Starting when I was fourteen, I spent every summer at a sleepaway camp for Jewish kids in the Santa Monica Mountains. I hated it at first. I was a bit of a late bloomer and it horrified me to have to use communal bathrooms and showers with my bunkmates, many of whom had full tufts of hair on their balls and under their arms, which stood in stark contrast to my slight, wiry, body-hair-less frame. Many of the guys were from well-to-do families—the sons of doctors and lawyers in Beverly Hills or Pacific Palisades. The kids dressed in the hippest of wardrobes, and had practically been pre-enrolled at birth at Berkeley or Michigan or USC. I was just a middle-class kid in middle-class clothes, and I therefore felt as inferior socially as I did physically. While the other guys were dressing in their very *Miami Vice* attire—an expensive pastel-colored T-shirt under a white suit coat—and drowning themselves in Drakkar Noir cologne, I wore whatever we could get from Ross Dress for Less. It was clear that we were from different sides of the mall, and I felt like an outcast because of it. I wanted to be like them. They seemed so mature, so self-assured. They knew how to act, how to get girls to like them, how to play the game. Their confidence and cockiness bordered on arrogance, and although I was disturbed by it at times, I thirsted to be that sure of myself. I remember once asking a bunkmate if I could have a few squirts of his Polo cologne. He obliged, and that night in the dining hall one of the many cute Madonna look-alikes smelled it when she walked by.

"Danny! Are you wearing cologne?"

(She noticed!)

"Yeah," I said bashfully. "It's Polo."

It was her turn to speak, and in the second or two before she did I convinced myself that her response would set the course for the rest of my life. Did I actually have any possibility of attracting a girl or was I destined to spend the rest of my life playing Atari Missile Command in my room at my parents' house? It was up to her.

She laughed. She thought I had worn that cologne as a joke, as a parody of myself. I was a nerd, and there's just something hilarious about a nerd wearing cologne. Think about it. People adorn themselves with fragrances as part of a whole ensemble designed to convey sexuality and attractiveness. But given that there's very little else about a nerd that communicates those messages, the aroma of sex is enormously out of place. It's like putting a pocket protector on a supermodel; doesn't work at all.

Naturally, I was crushed. But as time waned on and I grew more comfortable with the environment and its inhabitants, my ability to make the other people laugh became the great equalizer. They accepted me as one of their friends, and I soon developed a reputation as the funniest kid in camp. I was a novelty. I loved the acceptance and attention it brought me. Laughter was approval. Validation. Wow! But behind the omnipresent smile on my face was the mind of a real adolescent boy. I wanted to kiss a girl. I wanted to hold hands and pass notes and know that there would be someone to sit next to at the campfire. As much as I liked making the girls laugh and giggle, the friendships I had with them had a finite level of depth and connection. It was difficult to take seriously the guy who was never serious. They saw me as a clown, not a regular boy, but I kept joking around because I'd worked hard to get their attention and I wasn't going to let some stupid hurt feelings blow that for me.*

This cycle repeated itself over and over. I lived in the on-campus dorms during my first year at Fresno State, and word soon made its way through the halls that the skinny guy on the first floor of Graves Hall was hilarious. Again, I was invited into the brotherhood because I could make the others laugh. My buddies and I developed a Tuesday night tradition called

---

* This is not to say I was a total failure with the ladies. By some stroke of good fortune, three different girls saw fit to kiss me by the time I graduated college. One even referred to me as her boyfriend. But as each of these poor, misguided girls could attest, I had no idea how to kiss a girl. Where do you put your tongue? What do you do with all of the slobber? How do you know when it's okay to start touching things? In true nerd fashion, I figured there must be some sort of textbook on the subject, some literary guide to navigating romantic awkwardness, but I never found one. Through trial and error (mostly error) I managed to find my way around a woman without being slapped, pepper-sprayed, or incarcerated.

"Family Night," during which we would gather in one of the dorm rooms, drink cheap beer, scarf bad pizza, and watch porn. I loved the camaraderie, and the guys loved having me there because I could always be counted on for a hilarious or crude comment about one of the people on-screen. My friend Bill was particularly enamored of a starlet named Tori Welles, a brunette with a pierced nostril and a voracious appetite for cock. We rented a lot of Tori's movies, and Bill was fond of pausing the film whenever there was a close-up of her most private of places. During one particular scene, Tori's partner was in the midst of performing cunnilingus when he placed his thumbs on either side of her crotch and spread it apart. It left absolutely nothing to the imagination.

"Jesus fucking Christ!" I shouted. "Is he trying to see what she ate for lunch?"

The room erupted in laughter. It felt awesome. They howled, and that summoned in me a powerful feeling of self-satisfaction and glee. I was one of the guys. But the vibe changed significantly on nights when there were girls around. One night after we'd all been drinking beer, I followed the guys up to a room on the third floor. When we arrived, each of my buddies dispersed to locations around the room where their girlfriends were sitting on the floor or lying on a bed. Within seconds, I was standing alone under the doorframe. It was one of the loneliest moments of my life, and although I was feeling terrible about myself, I did what came naturally: I started telling jokes. The scene was reminiscent of a comedy club, complete with couples huddled around the audience, canoodling and loving on one another while the guy onstage makes an ass of himself. *"Ha! Look at the funny monkey dancing! Oh, my God, that's hilarious! Now let's make out."*

All my life I have used humor as a distraction from basic human emotions—sadness, fear, shame, anger—and by doing so I prevented myself from learning how to deal with those feelings appropriately. Though I was attempting to protect myself, every time I failed to engage the authenticity of my feelings I took another step toward depression. And when the sadness (9/11), fear (fatherhood), and shame (job loss) converged upon me almost simultaneously, I was emotionally defenseless. I lost my ability to see humor in life and I was unable to cope. I think Susan knew this about me instinctively and her failure to laugh at my jokes during therapy was her way of telling me it was time to stop running from what was real. It was time to look into the eyes of these distinctly unfunny emotions, feel them, get to know them.

The previous job safety discussion lit up like a flare for Susan, and her pursuit of the reason for my focus on it turned my world on its ass. She prodded me. What was I scared of? Why had I chosen safety at the expense of fulfillment? I had never questioned these things before. I didn't recall having made a choice or a decision to think that way. It was just who I was. But Susan had an extraordinarily low tolerance for bullshit and "I don't know" and other declarations that the issues at hand were too frightening or painful to examine. She ostensibly pushed me into a dark room, slammed the door behind me, and declared that I couldn't come out until I had done the work. Given my strong visceral need for approval, I was not hard to convince.

Just as she wouldn't let me hide from my issues, neither would Susan spoon-feed me. She forced me to make my own discoveries, although she certainly did adjust my sails in such a way that I'd float in their general direction. And by juxtaposing conversations about my career frustration and the fear I felt in response to my dad's ire, she led me to an extraordinary personal discovery: I was afraid to live my life on my own terms. I had never allowed myself to make my own choices because I was afraid of the anger, afraid that deviation from the safe path my parents wanted me to follow would end badly for me.

In my mind I pictured a dog wearing a shock collar. Every time it attempts to leave the yard, it gets jolted. The jolts hurt, and no matter how badly the dog wants to cruise around the neighborhood and sniff the asses of the other dogs, he eventually learns to scuttle those desires so as to avoid the painful shocks. I stayed in the yard, too, as did my emotional maturity. It hurt. So to make the sting hurt less I started to pretend it wasn't there. Always laughing, always joking, always coming up with something funny to say so as not to have to feel that sting. I stayed in my yard, cracked my jokes, stuffed my pain down my throat, and tried to forget it was there. But it *was* there. It was always there, festering inside the places in my mind where I dared not go. And when things got tougher than they'd ever been for me, out it came. All of it. The tears, the shame, the anger, the sadness, the what-ifs, the realizations. And for the first time in my life, I couldn't find anything funny to say.

"What is it?" Susan asked. Whether it was because of my transparency or her perceptiveness, she could always tell when a memory came into my consciousness.

"Once when I was a teenager, a relative of one of my buddies invited three of us to work on election night," I said. "I can't recall what our specific duties were— something to do with transporting ballots—but I remember we were standing in a big parking lot behind a post office in Van Nuys when this big, loud helicopter flew in and landed right there in the parking lot. The pilot gets out of the chopper, loads some big boxes into the back, and then he comes over to us and starts talking. It was actually yelling, so he could be heard over the loud hum of the copter blades, just like Duvall did in *Apocalypse Now*. So the pilot yells, 'Hey, I've got two empty seats on the copter if any of you guys want to go.' And I remember that my first thought—even before I considered how incredible it would be to fly in a helicopter—was that I absolutely couldn't do it. There was just no way."

"I think I could have predicted that," Susan said. She wasn't being snarky or flippant; she'd heard enough of my stories to know what my reactions would be in certain situations. "Go on."

"I was paralyzed, Susan. I felt in my bones that it wouldn't be okay. I thought about my folks and what they would have said if I came home and told them I'd ridden in a helicopter. I think they would have been furious with me. And if I had just gone, I would have been so ridden with angst the whole time that I couldn't possibly have enjoyed it. But then, before I could even finish these thoughts, the other two guys I was with stepped forward and said yes."

My eyes welled up. I was stewing in frustration.

"Where are those tears coming from?" Susan asked.

"I just . . . I remember watching that stupid helicopter lift off the ground and fly away and I just felt so . . . you know . . . so small. Why was it so easy for the two other guys to raise their hands? Why was it so hard for me?"

Susan leaned forward and handed me a tissue. I took it but held it in my lap. This wasn't the first time I had shed tears in front of a therapist, but it never before felt like this. There was something I liked about feeling tears run down my face and watching them land on my shirt. It was evidence. I didn't want to wipe them away because I wasn't done feeling them yet.

"And when the guys came back in the helicopter, they were crazy excited, you know? Out of their minds. They were telling me about how they'd flown over

Dodger Stadium and downtown L.A. They saw the Hollywood Bowl. Totally a once-in-a-lifetime experience."

I wiped my nose with the tissue and then dabbed my eyes, feeling as I did so that this wound had been opened far enough. I was ready to think about something else. But I'd spent enough time with Susan to know she wouldn't let me off until the helicopter topic had been exhaustively examined and picked clean. I thank her for that. I learned in therapy with her that if something feels difficult or uncomfortable to discuss, it's too important to leave alone. It's supposed to be hard. I often hear guys tell me they don't believe therapy would work or that they flatly don't need it, and I can't help but believe that some of them are merely trying to camouflage their anxiety that it *will* work and they won't know how to deal with what they discover about themselves. I understand that fear. I've felt it myself. But I've also felt the way my chest seems to deflate and how my shoulder muscles involuntarily relax after I've allowed myself to dig deep and expose my soul for my own benefit. The latter is so much more satisfying than the former. It's quite something to walk out of a therapy session with a feeling that you actually accomplished something.

"Man," I said after a lengthy, deafening pause. "I've been holding that in for a long time."

"How does it feel to get it off your chest?"

I answered her question by exhaling completely and relaxing my muscles all the way to rag doll mode. "It kind of surprised me."

"How so?"

"It's just weird that I hadn't thought about that incident in, what, fifteen years?" I said. "But today I remembered it with such clarity that I could tell you exactly how I felt in that moment. That paralysis. What does that even mean?"

"What do *you* think it means?" she asked.

"Well, I suppose it means it was important to me in some developmental way."

"Keep going."

"Hmm. Well. It's . . . it's almost as though there were two parts of my brain fighting with one another. There was the part that I had lived with since I was a little kid—the part that wanted to please everyone and stay within the safe zone. But there was a more mature version of me trying to take over, trying to live my life on my own terms, which meant pouncing on that opportunity to ride in a helicopter and just generally do what I wanted to do."

"You were growing up."

"But I guess the young me won that day," I said.

"It's still winning," she said. "We've only just begun to set you straight."

NINETEEN

Although it was difficult and sometimes very uncomfortable to have to pick apart my own brain in therapy—a process Peter Gabriel called "digging in the dirt"—to try to locate the pain in my mind, there was something satisfying about it, too. I got to know myself. It's quite something to sit on a couch and just talk, for an hour, and have someone across from you listen, interpret, and assist in that personal analysis. Privacy is implicit and the only boundaries of conversation are those that existed in my own mind. I could talk about anything. I could cry. I could take my deepest, darkest thoughts out of my own head and actually speak them to someone, which for some reason always felt like a remarkable relief. Almost every time I left Susan's office, I did so feeling physically different than when I'd gone in, as though my soul had exhaled. My breathing eased. My entire being felt as though it had just gone through a vigorous deep tissue massage at the fingers of a hearty Swedish woman with the hands of an all-pro linebacker. On days when I just wasn't into going to therapy, when I wanted not to be exposed to myself, that feeling of release was what made me go to my appointment anyway.

The more we discussed my depression and the causes thereof, the more my relationship with my father came into view. I found it difficult to examine, partly because I knew there was a lot of hurt in that topic, but also because I felt a strong need to protect my dad. Beyond the fact that he was aging and in declining health, I'd heard a sufficient number of stories from my mom to know that he'd endured a downright awful childhood. I didn't want to make him vulnerable to any more heartache. I didn't want him to have to relive those moments, even if it meant that I might heal my soul.

My dad was born during World War II in Altoona, Pennsylvania, a smoky little city whose growth and economy was inexorably linked to the burgeoning Pennsylvania Railroad. Until steam locomotive construction halted there in 1946 and redirected the city's rail workforce from manufacturing to a focus on repair and maintenance, the railroad's Altoona Works complex employed around fifteen thousand people, including my grandfather.

By all outward appearances, my dad's youth was gloriously ordinary. Summer days meant building forts in the foothills of the Alleghenies and playing cowboys and Indians with his buddies. Guns were made of a fist, an outstretched index finger, and an upright thumb. *Peew-peew!* When killed in action by a dirt-clod grenade, death lasted only long enough to catch one's breath and wipe the dirt from one's knees. In the winter, he rode his sled down those same hills, pretending to be aboard a rocket ship or an American B-17 "Flying Fortress" raining bloody hell on the German U-boats thousands of feet below. The adventures in the foothills were so fierce, so perfectly boyish, that my dad only stopped playing long enough to return home for meals and occasionally to change his socks, which routinely became soiled to near blackness by the thick, omnipresent filth belched into the air by the locomotives.

But my dad's penchant for all things outdoors was as much about sanctuary and self-preservation as it was having fun. Outside he was safe. Outside there was no one to humiliate him, no one to make him feel small. He lived in a modest two-story structure built by his dad. There was a pair of bedrooms and a kitchen–dining room on the first story and a third bedroom upstairs. The second floor was what we would nowadays call a "clusterfuck." It wasn't so much a room as it was two bookends of space that sandwiched a big void where the stairway ascended to the second story. There was only enough space on one side of the staircase for a bed and a nightstand, and a small bathroom on the opposite side. That was my dad's room.

I'm not comfortable declaring that my grandparents didn't love my dad or didn't want him, but it's quite clear that they didn't like him or respect him. Circumstantial evidence that proves such a terrible thing abounds—some of it in my dad's head, some in mine. My dad is a tall, quiet, stoic man. The women at Temple Jewey Jew-Jew used to call him "the gentle giant" because beneath his six-feet-four frame is a kind, generous man. They were right, of course. But there was another side to him that they didn't see. The side he kept from them. The side that surely evolved as a result of his toxic relationship with his parents. I suppose there's only so many times a boy can be humiliated and only so long he can be made to feel unworthy of his parents' love before a part of his heart hardens. Before it decides to defend itself.

One day when my dad was about ten, he came home from school to find that his parents had rented his room to a stranger and relegated my dad to a creaky metal cot in the hallway downstairs. They never told him why, never showed him any sympathy. His family is gone now, so he has no way of knowing exactly why he was cast out so abruptly and resoundingly, but he assumes it was for financial reasons. While that sounds reasonable, there's a part of me that can't help but think he made that up to protect himself.

The tie that most inexorably links me to my father is control—or in some cases, the lack thereof. As a child, he had none. He was manipulated and moved around like a pawn, existing in an interminable state of unease. Even when he *was* at home, my dad lived in fear of the Paddle: an eighteen-inch-long pine swatter with an eight-inch handle. The Paddle had my dad's name on one side and his sister's on the other. It was menacingly kept in a kitchen drawer and treated by his mother as a means by which to taunt him and a source of crass humor, but it was no joke to my dad. (He told me his dad never used it on him, but when I asked him if his mom ever did, he declined to answer "because you shouldn't speak evil about the dead.") The volatility and confusion engrained in him by the circumstances of his childhood naturally conditioned my dad to believe that someday, when he was finally able to escape the psychological clutches of his parents, he would establish control over his own existence. And like a virus growing in a laboratory, the control needed a host—an environment or emotional state of being wherein the virus of control would live and breathe and run free. Think of the workaholic, the overzealous Little League dad, the relentless beauty pageant mom who throws a conniption at the mere suggestion of an out-of-place sequin on her daughter's gown. These characters and many like them achieve a semblance of order in their lives with practically dictatorial domination of their business or their children.

In my case, there were two hosts. Beyond his application of the Little League dad behavior on my Jewish education, there was also the anger. Whether this volatility was a relic of his own parents' behavior or his own contribution to the emotional soup that served as my genetic inheritance, the course of my life was very much determined by my father and enforced by his anger. There was a certain person he wanted me to be, and any action I took in contradiction to that version of Danny was repelled or squashed by the frightening voice of my father. I was terrified into compliance, and because my father determined that I was going to be a learned Jewish scholar (as opposed to the athletic, professional baseball player I imagined myself to be), I was essentially strong-armed toward a behavioral inclination that dogged me well into adulthood: I was a nerd of the highest order. And that was a tough way to live.

The hours of therapy and intense self-evaluation with Susan made clear to me that there was a prevailing element of victimization in my life. Considering my father's upbringing and the consistency with which he was the victim of insensitivity and disrespect, it makes sense that we had in common the idea that those around us determined our self-worth. I ultimately found the absurdity in that outlook and learned to repel it, but not until I was in my midthirties. Had I learned to rebel and rage against the *meshugenah* as a child, I might have avoided some of the humiliating victimization I encountered in school.

TWENTY

One morning in ninth grade, Eugene Ellerbe stabbed me in the gut with a mechanical pencil. Pretty hard-core pugnacity for a meek towheaded little dweeb like Eugene, whose fiercest act of aggression theretofore had been wiping a booger on Bruno DeMattia's backpack after Bruno broke Eugene's high score on Donkey Kong. That's how we used to settle things in the geek squad: boogers and loogies and wet willies. I suppose that's what made Eugene's attack so spectacular. Notwithstanding the simple fact that his Crown pencil pierced the skin on my abdomen and left behind a half-inch souvenir of busted lead, the real shock was the uncharacteristic bloodlust and hostility displayed by a kid who couldn't move a muscle without first taking a hit from his asthma inhaler.

We had a substitute teacher in computer science class that day, which typically portended bad things for the nerds. Back then we learned how to write computer programs on monolithic black terminals called TRS-80s (everyone called them Trash 80s). There were two dozen of them in the computer lab—a small, poorly ventilated, portable building planted next to the teachers' parking lot—and everyone who used the "Trashers" knew about their logic-defying design flaw: a small square button on the top right corner of the keyboard. The kill switch. If pressed, the button shut down the computer and whatever data hadn't been saved was lost forever. There were very few cool kids in computer class, but those who were enrolled developed a fun little game called "Let's Piss Off the Nerds and Laugh at Their Impotent Rage," during which they would sneak up behind us and push the kill switch in the middle of our projects. Because they knew none of us had the muscle mass or intestinal fortitude to stand up to them, the sight of a substitute teacher was like Christmas morning for the jocks, stoners, and class clowns.

Eugene was the chosen mark that morning because he was the geek most intently concentrating on his work. The ideal target for a sneak attack. One after another, for almost the entire hour, they crept up behind Eugene, heartlessly killed his machine, and scooted back to their seats before the substitute teacher awoke from her gin-induced slumber. The rest of us dweebs were so overjoyed to have escaped this wrath that we began to laugh as hard at Eugene's misfortune as the other kids. There's nothing funnier than an angry nerd.

"Hey. Evans."

It was Gabe Gilbert, the boy rumored to have touched the boob of Ashley Vincent, the cheerleader every nerd in school would have given his most prized Dungeons and Dragons dice just to talk to. Gabe had never spoken to me (I didn't even know he knew my name), so I perked up immediately to claim my validation.

"Yeah, Gabe?"

"Go kill Ellerbe's computer or I'll kick your ass."

My heart sank. Eugene was my friend. We'd gotten our braces at about the same time and we'd both suffered the ultimate indignity of having to wear our headgear to school. We had a running lunchtime agreement that I would trade him my Del Monte fruit cup for his Cheetos. But what choice did I have here? In my panic, I calculated that I stood a better chance of Eugene forgiving me than I did of surviving a beating by Gabe.

"Okay, Gabe. I'll do it."

I stood from my chair and began to sneak toward Eugene's computer, looking back with each step to make sure Gabe and his boys were still watching. I was wearing my light blue corduroy pants that day and I remember worrying that the *vit-vit* sound of the rubbing ridges would alert Eugene to my presence. But when I got to within just a step or two, I was still confident that I hadn't been noticed. I paused for a moment and swiveled my glance back to Gabe, hoping against all hope that he'd call off the attack. Maybe he was just testing me to see if I was man enough to get out of the chair, and since I demonstrated at least a modicum of balls, I was free to come over to his house for lasagna and to feel up Ashley Vincent for dessert. But there was no such cease-fire. He mouthed the words "Do it, nerd" and flicked the back of his hand a couple of times—the universal sign for "go ahead."

I turned around, took a breath, and lunged toward Eugene's kill switch. At that very instant Eugene grabbed his pencil, wheeled around in his chair, and drove the lead into my right side, perfectly placed in the hollow between two ribs. The room erupted in oohs and aahs, and in an instant Eugene became a cult hero on campus (not unlike the tragically untalented guy laughed off of the TV singing competition only to become a celebrity for his tone deafness). Gabe never talked to me again after that and I never got to lay a single quivering finger on Ashley. But I did get to leave school early that day. To get a tetanus shot.

You never recover from something like that. Nerds start out with a severe street cred deficit as it is, but I learned that year that it's possible to retreat even further from coolness. Even the other members of the geek squad chose not to associate with me, and trust me: you haven't known sorrow until kids with dandruff, pocket protectors, and a tendency to snort when they laugh think you're beneath them. When ninth grade finally drew to an end and the school yearbook came out, I was voted "Most Likely to Die Without Ever Having Kissed a Girl That Wasn't His Mom."

TWENTY-ONE

As a man in his early thirties, I felt like quite a namby-pamby sitting across from Susan and describing for her the ways I was controlled as a boy. It's not natural. I felt as though I should be telling her how I rose up and fought for what I wanted, what I believed in, what I knew was right. That's what a man would do. A man would not have allowed himself to be stabbed with a pencil. A man would not have been disrespected or scared. And even if those things had happened when he was a boy, a man would have gotten over it by now. "Fuck 'em," he'd say. "Fuck 'em all." But depression has a way of making that stereotypical male bravado look pretty silly. It strips away the chaps and the five o'clock shadow and cowboy hat, leaving the Marlboro Man standing there disarmed and exposed for what he is under that gruff exterior: a human being. Like everyone else, he hurts. He fails. He falls on his ass. What good does it do him to deny that? Where's the glory in ignoring pain? It seemed to me that stomping through life without addressing what hurt me was no different than that cowboy smoking cigarettes all his life. In either case, you're a fool to believe it won't catch up to you eventually.

So I succumbed. I gave myself up to the process and allowed myself to shine the harsh light of self-examination on everything—including the experiences and emotions that I feared would "harm" my dad or injure his feelings. Knowing his thirst for learning Torah and mathematical principles, I trusted that he would understand my need to understand my childhood for the sake of helping myself, not assigning blame or directing pent-up rage at him. Parenthood helped me clear that up in my own mind. Just as I was doing with Noah, he had done his best to raise Debbie and me. He was committed. But you come at fatherhood with your own emotional perspective, having learned what a father should look like based on the example of your own. This is not to say that my father's behaviors were not his own fault, but simply to let him off the hook. He tried. He succeeded in many ways. But now it was incumbent upon me to take over the captaincy of my own ship.

It would be easier to throw up one's hands and say my grandparents flatly didn't know how to raise a child or didn't know how to love. I think my dad could find some solace in that. But it's not true. My aunt Sarah was two years my dad's junior, and there is no need to mince words about this: she was her parents' favored child. While my dad was overlooked, Sarah was showered with heaps of praise and attention and love. I witnessed it with my own eyes. I was treated similarly, but only briefly.

When we were kids, my grandmother lavished Sarah and her kids with gifts and kisses and "Oh, aren't they just so wonderful!" while virtually ignoring Debbie and me. Debbie and I couldn't have cared less about the emotional support, but the clear disparity in material possessions pissed us off. We were confused by it. Had we done something wrong? Why didn't grandma like us? Fortunately for Debbie and me, we were a generation removed from her favoritism and we had our mom to explain it to us. To borrow an expression from my dad, our grandma's elevator didn't go all the way to the top.

A decade or so later, Sarah went into therapy after her husband abandoned his family for Sarah's best friend, and the experience predictably brought a hailstorm of troubling memories and feelings into the front row of her consciousness. Those memories were magnified when she developed leukemia. My dad was a perfect match to donate bone marrow for her transplant, and the selflessness of his gesture summoned within Sarah a feeling of connectedness with him. For the first time. My dad was in his fifties.

She came to our house one Saturday afternoon—which itself was quite rare since she and my dad were not close—and sat at our dining room table sipping Sanka with my parents.

"I have to ask you something," Sarah said to my dad. "This therapist I'm seeing asked me last week if I could recall ever having a playdate with friends or a birthday party. I can't. I honestly can't remember ever having such a thing. Can you?"

My dad bowed his head and stared blankly into his coffee cup, as if all of the world's answers were buried beneath that brew.

"I can't either," he said. His voice sounded resigned. Defeated. He sounded that way whenever he talked about the past.

According to my wife, so do I.

When my dad was in eighth grade, his parents withdrew him from school and sent him to live with his grandparents in Chicago. As was their pattern, they never told him why. But my dad was a pretty sharp kid. He figured it out himself.

He remembers hearing the term "nervous breakdown" being used a lot in reference to my grandmother. The friends to whom she would tell grandiose stories about Sarah's frequent triumphs whispered the term to one another loud enough for my dad to hear, especially in the months that preceded his unexplained exile to Chicago. *Nervous breakdown.* That's the term people used back then—back before they knew why it happens, how it feels, or what it does to a person. We're a lot more knowledgeable about it now, and we call it something else.

We call it depression.

Heredity plays a role in depression, just as it does with other diseases. Having a depressed parent makes one more likely to suffer from depression, and there is an abundance of evidence in my own familial history to bear this out. At its core, the depression that afflicted my father and grandmother is no different from my own, but it's fascinating to me to consider how confrontation (or lack thereof) of the disease has changed from one generation to the next while the cultural acceptance and understanding of depression has remained at a virtual standstill.

In the 1950s, my grandmother's nervous breakdown was fodder for whispers and conjecture because no one around her was quite sure what it meant, what she might do, or what having such a friend said about them. My "breakdown" occurred more than fifty years later, at a time when public perception of mental illness in general has matured somewhat (thanks to celebrity postpartum depression memoirs and popular films like *One Flew Over the Cuckoo's Nest* and *Girl, Interrupted*). Despite the collateral damage that altered my father's youth, I feel a tinge of empathy for my grandmother because the collective ignorance about her ailment at the time it occurred must have exponentially worsened the ordeal. I have wondered what might have become of my life had I been born just two generations earlier—before there were television commercials for antidepressant medications and mental health professionals on every street corner. Would I have been shunned? Would I have been blackballed? Would I have been able to come to my own defense?

TWENTY-TWO

Sharon and I agreed very early in our courtship that if we ever got married and had kids, we would raise them "Jewishly." I was more than happy to agree to such an arrangement back then because I had grown up in a Jewish environment, and despite my inflamed point of view on the religious tentacles of the faith, I was comfortable and content around Jewish people, Jewish food, Jewish tchotchkes, and the unique vernacular of the American Jewish population. In 1993, when Sharon and I discussed the issue, it was easy to agree because it was merely a concept. There was no engagement yet, meaning no marriage, and certainly no kids. There was the future, and like so many other nebulous and challenging predicaments I've encountered in my life, I cast it aside for the time being and pledged to deal with it when the appropriate time came.

About a decade later, the time came. Noah had reached the age that was suitable for introducing him to Judaism, and that meant officially "joining" a synagogue. Sharon signed us up as members of the temple to which she and her family belonged in her youth. It was close to our house, close to her heart, and extremely far away (in proximity and intensity) from the temple of *my* youth. Still, I was made uncomfortable even by the prospect of again having to attend lengthy services, listening to people spew awestricken gibberish about a God I didn't believe in, while I sat there trying not to prejudice the thinking of my son. In this domain, perhaps more than any other facet of his life, I wanted him to feel free. My goal was to show him a structure upon which faith and belief could be built, but I was determined not to force-feed him the precise specifications and building codes he'd need to construct his own. In fact, I have found specifically that balancing act—teaching my kids to make smart decisions without coloring their thinking with my own biases—to be the most challenging part of parenthood. For that reason, I saw providing Noah an entrée to Judaism was fraught with inner conflict for me. I proceeded with extreme caution.

Speaking of biases, I'm extraordinarily possessive of my Saturday mornings nowadays. I try not to make any plans or commitments because this one part of my week is sacred to me, and I treasure it dearly. I'm certain my psychotic, irrational stance on this issue is related to the Saturday mornings of my youth, which were not at all my own. See, we attended Shabbat morning services every Saturday—a weekly, three-hour torture method that compares favorably with having one's limbs ripped and pecked from his torso with a spork. Because my parents were so zealous about their desire to make me the world's first perfect Jew, if I come within one mile of a synagogue my throat closes up and I break into hives in the shape of a Star of David. I bore this overzealousness in mind when I looked at the chosen pursuit of my own son, lest I sour his passionate, all-consuming love for baseball. But sometimes it's hard for me to contain my own enthusiasm for the game, which merely serves to fuel the boy's love. That poses a problem. I want there to be balance and variety in his life, and yet there is none in my own life when it comes to baseball. Baseball is life and breath. It is the sun and the moon and the stars. In fact, as I have examined this very delicate part of parenthood, it has occurred to me that if the faith into which I was born had merely adopted a small sampling of my favorite subtleties from the game of baseball, I could return to the temple with open arms and an open mind. For example:

1. Heckling should be permitted at services.
There's nothing like being at a ballgame and, after the opposing right fielder has dropped an easily catchable pop fly, hollering out to him, "Hey, you big sissy, catch

it in your purse next time!" That would translate seam-lessly to Saturday morning services when, after the rabbi fumbles over a difficult-to-pronounce Hebrew word, I would stand up in my pew and shout, "Hey, rabbi! Pull your head out! It's *'ah-doe-nye,'* not *'ah-do-nay-nee-hoo!'* That crap might work in the minors, but you're in the big time now!"

2. Concession stands would do wonders for the enjoyment of temple congregants.

Jews love to eat, and there's just something about see-ing the Torah that makes me want some nachos or a Slushie or a package of Red Vines. The concession stand will need to sell $8 cups of watered-down Mani-schewitz wine instead of watered-down beer, but just like at the ballgame, people will probably sneak their own brew into services by hiding it in their purses.

3. Male rabbis, like ballplayers, should have to wear a protective cup.

You never know when an errant matzoh ball is going to shoot down from the heavens and bean someone right in his holy Hebrew National. Better safe, that's all I'm sayin'.

4. There should be an umpire at services.

The rabbi is speaking mostly Hebrew and none of us poor, dumb saps in the congregation would have any clue if he was cheesing around with the rules, perhaps mixing in some Swahili or something. In Judaism, there are rules. And when those rules are broken, people die.

5. In baseball, when someone goes beyond the boundaries of simple obnoxiousness or insubordination, they get thrown out of the game. This clearly needs to be adopted by the synagogue.

I'm thinking of a certain member of our temple, a woman whose singing voice rivals the estrus-drunk howl of a wildebeest. I would like nothing better than to see the rabbi waltz up to her, take off her yarmulke, squeeze his nose right up against hers, and yell, "Oh yeah?! *Oh yeah?! WELL, YOU'RE OUTTA HERE, LADY! SHALOM!*"

As a father, I was at my best during prayer services at the synagogue. When Noah *kvetched* or became restless or needed to pee, I gleefully volunteered to remove him from the sanctuary and tend to his needs. The glee came from the fact that *I* got to leave the room, too, thereby saving myself from the torture of interminable rote repetition of variations of the same prayer. *God kicks ass. Asses, You kick them, God. Hear, O Israel, thine asses hath been kickethed by God.* Noah and I usually made our stealth escape to a small foyer near the front entrance of the temple—a confused, schizophrenic space comprised of equal parts seating area, Judaica gift shop, memorial wall, and reception desk. Not surprisingly, Noah and I weren't the only father–fidgety child duo in the room, and my bond with the other dads grew closer with each passing Shabbat, Purim, and Yom Kippur. For the first time in my adult life, I went to the temple with an emotional posture other than pure dread. I actually looked forward to going, which is as crazy as . . . as . . . *as a fiddler! On the roof!*

While our children spent their time turning on and off the lightbulbs next to the name plaques on the memorial wall, my new friends and I got to know each other better. What the guys in the group lacked in eclectic backgrounds—four of them were lawyers with conservative political leanings, and many were born and raised in this neighborhood and had been Bar Mitzvahed in this synagogue—was more than compensated for with their senses of humor and their allegiances to the same sports teams for which I rooted (notably the Anaheim Angels, the Anaheim Ducks, and the Los Angeles Lakers).

Josh was one of the lawyers, although he'd interrupt any such generalized reference to himself with a reminder that he was deputy district attorney, not some slimy ambulance chaser. "I do God's work," he said, a claim that had a lot of its thunder robbed in broad daylight by Josh's short frame and sports illiteracy. He had no chest to stick out when he said it, no real swagger about himself, either. Josh was one of the few people I've ever known who uses more profanity than I do, but his potty mouth belied a genuine sensitivity and vulnerability that simmered beneath his words when we talked. There was something about him with which I connected shortly after we met, but I couldn't place exactly what it was at first.

I wasn't myself that afternoon in the temple lobby. The depression I'd been working so hard to keep at bay occasionally found its way over the moat I'd built with therapy and meds, and I suppose that was evident in my demeanor. Or perhaps on my face. Either way, Josh approached me in a quiet corner of the foyer, where I was mindlessly eyeballing the crystal candlesticks for sale at the gift shop.

"What's the matter," he asked, "you couldn't afford the one on QVC?"

I obliged with a chuckle and a forced smile.

"Everything okay?" His tone was different. Less playful.

"Eh."

"Eh? What's 'Eh'?"

I thought for a split second about not telling him—about evading the question as I had dozens of times before. You can never predict how another guy will react, and that unknown caused me enough fear to keep the depression to myself. But I was tired of hiding, and just as I had stepped out of the shadows to confront the disease itself head-on, I decided in that pause that it was time to do the same with the ridiculous social stigma from which I was cowering.

"I'm depressed, Josh."

"What about?" He looked confused.

"Not about anything in particular. Not that kind of depressed. I have what the shrinks call 'clinical depression.'"

As soon as the words left my mouth I scanned Josh's face for a reaction. Would he be repulsed? Would he take a step backward? On the contrary. Josh involuntarily squinted, contorting his brow in a way I knew to mean he wanted to know more. There was no repulsion, no summary judgment, only intellectual curiosity. I told Josh everything—layoff, 9/11, drinking, therapy, meds—and the more I revealed, the more relief I felt to finally be shedding it. I once heard Lenny Kravitz, one of my favorite musicians of the 1990s, describe the sensation of cutting off the dreadlocks he'd worn for much of his adult life. As each lock of hair was cut, Lenny said, he involuntarily took deep breaths and felt "lighter" with each exhalation, as though the dreads had weighed him down and the haircut was relieving him of the oppressive burden. The experience of unloading my story to Josh elicited a similar emotional relief within me. I felt the tightness in my neck and shoulders releasing. I felt my chest and forehead relax. The simple act of saying aloud what I had not felt safe sharing with anyone but my wife and my therapist provided for me a release I could never have expected. More important, it helped me to realize I was not alone.

Befitting a crafty attorney ("God's work," my ass), Josh let me finish my whole depression monologue before sharing that he too had suffered from the disease after his son Gabriel was diagnosed with an autism spectrum disorder. Predictably, Josh was careful about the way he made this disclosure, doing so over the course of three conversations and refraining from exposing the gory details of his struggle. Nonetheless, Josh was my first depression buddy—but certainly not my last. I learned over the subsequent months that depression among men is extraordinarily prevalent, so much so that it defies categorization into a neat little socioeconomic, racial, or ethnic package. From CEOs with "golden parachutes" to unionized pipe fitters, there are men who suffer so mightily under the weight of life that their brains implode, causing these men to involuntarily throw up their hands and say, "I can't do this anymore." Worse still, this collapse usually happens in silence.

What's hard about depression is the sad but incontrovertible reality that you won't be better tomorrow. Or the next day. When you lie down to sleep, you do so with the knowledge that you will still be depressed when you awaken, and that's a pretty miserable way to live. You forget how it feels to be the way you were before you were depressed. How it feels to be normal. I began to look for small victories with which to distract myself from tomorrow, and from today. When my head hit the pillow, I closed my eyes and retraced my day (to the extent that I could remember it).

Did I make anyone laugh today?

Did I laugh today?

Did I feel any better today?

It worked sometimes, which is to say I drifted off with a warm thought in my head. But it was usually just another feeble exercise, just like my efforts to bond with my son, to connect with Sharon, to explain to people what was wrong with me.

I considered trying out for the track team during my sophomore year in high school. I had never actually attempted to run a distance longer than that I traversed from my front door to the ice cream man's truck three houses down our street, but I knew I was tall and skinny like all of the distance runners on the Olympics and that had to count for something, right? Actually, no. The first time I dared to brave an actual oval dirt track, I had my hands on my knees before a single lap. It hurt to breathe. I assumed at that moment that I simply lacked the stamina to endure something that long, that grueling, that intense.

Depression proved that hypothesis wrong. Recovery is a marathon. You stand at the starting line dressed in your fly Nike running gear. Your legs are muscular, your face awash with confidence and determination. *Pop!* The starter's pistol fires, but you can't move. The other runners take off past you, stepping around you, some of them cursing at your immobility. With your hands you grab your hamstring and physically move your right leg forward a step. It's infuriating. Has the asphalt turned to quicksand? Have your shoes turned to granite? Each day you take one step, and when that day is over, you're completely out of gas. It's hard, tedious labor. You want to quit. You want to give in to your exhaustion, to just lie down on the ground and let the heat radiating up from the asphalt burn your pain away. Why not just succumb? Wouldn't that be so much easier? Yes. Of course it would.

TWENTY-THREE

'm not fond of waking up. I like *being* awake, obviously, because that's when all the good sports are on TV. But the actual transition from sleep to alertness kind of bums me out. I like sleeping, and I happen to be pretty good at it, and the whole experience of opening my eyes, remembering who and where I am, and coming to grips with the reality that the acrobatic monkey sex I was just having with Sharon, Kate Winslet, and Jessica Biel in a cabana on a deserted beach in the middle of the Pacific was only a dream—well, that's all just too jarring if you ask me.

As one might imagine, mornings are to the depressed mind what that huge, bug-eyed, ugly dude from the *Goonies* is to celebrity sex dreams. It doesn't get much worse. Since sleep was sporadic at best and actual "rest" was a virtual impossibility during my depression, I dreaded the act of waking up because there was hardly anything from which to awaken. Getting out of bed meant another new day of malaise. Another quicksand marathon. Another day chained to the dark, dank dungeon of my brain, assuming that the new day would be a carbon copy of the grim day before, and the grim day before that. That was my expectation when I awoke on July 5, 2002. After a night spent spiritlessly celebrating America's independence with can after can of Bud Light (I knew from attending the AA meeting that I wasn't an alcoholic, so I took that as license to keep drinking), I was still alert enough at first light to remember to drink water so as not to add physical pain to the psychological woe to come. I shuffled into the bathroom, closed the door, and turned on the light. I had to squint through the glare, my eyes barely open, and I stepped to the sink, bent forward, and gulped mouthful after mouthful of water directly from the faucet.

I stood and put all my weight onto my arms, and as my eyes adjusted to the light I remember seeing my flexed triceps in my reflection in the mirror. (One of the underappreciated benefits of being an underweight pussy is the ease with which I could mistake muscle definition for actual strength.) I followed the lines in my arms down to my wrists, and in my peripheral vision I saw a linear white shape on the counter next to me. I turned my head to look at it directly: a white pregnancy test stick lay on the pristine white tile countertop, and a solid pink + was emblazoned near the rounded end.

Doubt. *It's probably from Noah. I know she kept it, as a souvenir.*

Relief. *Jesus. That scared the hell out of me. I thought she was pregnant again.*

Confusion. *Wait. Why would she have been looking at an old pregnancy test?*

Fear. *Oh, my God. Is this new? Is this real? Did she just do this?*

Disorientation. *What if it's real? What the hell am I going to do?*

I wheeled around to locate Sharon, and there she stood in the doorway.

"Congratulations," she said, her eyes struggling to see me through the bright bathroom lights. Her smile was genuine, her joy sincere, but there was a measure of pain behind her eyes. I knew why. Imagine attempting to share such wonderful, life-altering news with someone virtually incapable of happiness.

"So this is for real?"

She smiled, stepped forward, and wrapped her arms around my waist. "Yes, honey. It's real."

The emotional centers in my brain were not only awake for the first time in months, they were immediately thrust into overdrive. The news was at once spectacular and horrifying—spectacular for obvious reasons, but horrifying because I was not at that moment in the proper frame of mind or being to help bring a new child into the world. A father is strong and stoic.

He is focused, bulletproof, fit enough to rescue his family from a burning building, to disarm an intruder, to be strong for his wife in the event that something tragic happens during pregnancy or childbirth. I was not that man. I was depressed, unemployed, and uninsured. I was frail and broken.

"Wow. A baby."

"Yep," Sharon said. "Ready or not, here it comes."

"I'm not," I said.

"Me neither. But we don't have much choice."

"I'm scared," I said.

"Me too."

Depression is a perspective-free zone. There's no sense in looking for a bright side, no value in considering that others may be worse off, because in truth there *isn't* anyone else. The entirety of a depressed man's concentration is internal—*his* misery, *his* struggle, *his* fucked-up existence. But suddenly, after almost two years of pathetic solitary focus, there *was* someone else. There was the someone represented by that pink **+**. (It seemed to me that my unborn child was taking a cue from The Artist Formerly Known As Prince, brilliantly electing to be known as a symbol until such time as he or she could be given a gender-appropriate name. Sharon and I referred to the fetus as Plus, or The Artist Formerly Known As Oops.)

I spent more than two years trying to change the subject for myself. But no pill, no supplement, no aha moment in therapy had done for me during that desperate span what the tiny pink **+** did almost instantaneously that morning. More than ever, plus meant more. More than me. More than this. My days would no longer be just about me and all of the heavy, ugly crap inside me; there was a baby coming. A new life: hope, purpose. A clean slate from which to begin anew. Getting myself well no longer existed as an option; it was an absolute necessity. I wanted to be able to bring this new child into the world with every advantage available to him or her, and in my mind that began with me getting back to being Me.

TWENTY-FOUR

My notion of providing for my new child began with the staples of human existence: food, shelter, medicine. In my mind, that was the world's way of ordering me to finally get off my ass and find a job, so I hid in the passivity of Monster.com, where I could apply for what few available jobs the Web site could bring to the screen of my blue-accented clamshell iBook (dubbed "My First Laptop" by my technically savvy, PC-loyal brother-in-law) with no effort more strenuous than the click of a button. I searched for any position listed under the heading "writer". or "copywriter" in Southern California and hit the "apply now" link on the screen.

"What is it that you're looking for?" Sharon asked

as she looked over my shoulder at the grimly short list of available job opportunities.

"I don't think it matters," I said. "I see this as a two-step process. Step one is finding a job—*any* job—as long as it offers decent pay and health insurance. Step two will be finding something better."

"Define 'better.' "

"More money. More satisfying. Less 'job' and more 'career.' Better."

I think she wanted to discuss my plan more, but morning sickness prevented her from doing so. Saved by the barf.

Six weeks and more than fifty applications after I began searching for full-time work, a human resources representative invited me for a face-to-face interview in downtown Los Angeles. I accepted her invitation, but I didn't dare tell her that the odds of my accepting a full-time gig in downtown L.A. were infinitesimal. Though I was born and raised in Los Angeles, I'd been downtown only once in my life. When I told my parents I was going to propose to Sharon, they demanded that I let them take me to their jeweler in the "jewelry district" downtown, which happens to be in the same general vicinity of the "drunk dudes sleeping on the sidewalk" district, the "it totally smells like piss around here" district, and the "put your wallet in your front pocket" district. I spent months' salary on a diamond ring that afternoon, and on the way back to the car I vowed never to return to downtown L.A. If fear for one's life isn't a perfect deterrent for divorce, nothing is.

It took me ninety minutes to drive the forty miles from my house to the interview, which (speaking of fearing for one's life) took place in a small, sparsely decorated office on the forty-eighth floor of a fifty-story building. After an hour of conversation with the hiring manager, I came up with the following reasons why the job was not right for me at all:

1. The title was "marketing associate," clearly a huge step down from my directorial position at Outside the Box.
2. A 50 percent cut in pay.
3. To be at work by 8:00 a.m., I'd have to wake up at 5:00 a.m. to catch a train from Orange County to L.A.
4. The employer was a worldwide, narcissism-infected dung heap of a commercial real estate firm.
5. I'd have the chance to engage my lifelong fear of heights on a daily basis.

I'd followed the mandatory tourist protocols of voyaging to the top of the Empire State Building and Sears Tower on vacation trips, and those were white-knuckled, asshole-puckered experiences on their own. But I began to reflect upon those rides as innocuous as climbing a single flight of stairs the moment I realized the certain death I'd have to confront with my new job. To wit:

(a) Less than a year had passed since September

11, 2001. Those images were still fresh and vivid in my mind, and the thought of working in a fifty-story building smack-dab in the middle of a major metropolitan area sent my depressed imagination into fits of "this is how I'm going to die."

(b) Southern California is earthquake territory. Only seven years earlier, a six-point-something temblor in nearby Northridge, California, shook me out of my bed. I was hyperaware of the prediction that a quake along the San Andreas Fault was due at any moment—and when it hit, everything south of Fresno was going to be ripped free from its underpinnings and Frisbee'd out into the Pacific, where we would all sink to the bottom of the sea and be eaten by those fish from *Finding Nemo* that look like thyroid-sick piranhas wearing miners' headlamps. Or, in the case of someone at the top of a fifty-story building, crushed beneath 10 billion pounds of Post-it notes and dry erase markers and vacuum-sealed packages of microwave popcorn.

(c) *The Towering Inferno*. I considered myself to be a smidge more athletic than Ernie Borgnine, but I still wasn't sure I could make it down forty-eight flights of stairs without ending up like Michael Jackson did when filming that Pepsi commercial that went terribly awry.

Indeed, I would have been a fool to take the job. And were it not for The Artist Formerly Known As Oops, I would never have agreed to the interview. But I couldn't stop thinking about that tiny pink +.

I took the job.

(Have I mentioned that I was mentally ill?)

My direct supervisor was a snotty, uptight woman with a German accent, a name similar to that of a popular Swiss throat lozenge, and a stick so far up her ass that I could practically see it poking through the top of her scalp. I came into the job knowing I would be tasked with projects well below my capabilities, but I certainly did not expect to be talked down to or treated like an intern.

from *Danny Evans <dannyevans@commercialreal-estatefancypants.com>*
to *Helga The Unpleasant <htunpleasant@commercialrealestatefancypants.com>*
subject *Workload*

Hi Helga,
It looks as though you're particularly busy today and I wanted to let you know that I'm available to assist you in any way I can. I've completed my list of tasks for today, including proofreading, Xeroxing, and disseminating that hilarious Family Circus cartoon you thought everyone on the 47th, 48th and 49th floors would get a kick out of, so if there's any additional mindless busywork with which I can help, I'd be happy to pitch in.
Sincerely,
Danny Evans
Marketing Associate

P.S.—Everyone on the 47th, 48th and 49th floors thought that cartoon was lame and that it further cements your reputation as a humorless prima donna.

from *Helga The Unpleasant <htunpleasant@commercialrealestatefancypants.com>*
to *Danny Evans <dannyevans@commercialrealestatefancypants.com>*
subject *re: Workload*

Danny,
I am perfectly capable of managing my own workload, and I'll thank you not to assume that I need you to rescue me just because I am a woman and just because I am not from this country. In the future, please refrain from sticking your nose in where it doesn't belong. Just sit there and do the dumb marketing associate work I hired you to do—nothing more.
Sincerely,
Helga The Unpleasant
Worldwide Marketing Director
Obviously Better Than a Lowly Marketing Associate
Also, Very Threatened by Men
P.S.—The people who didn't like my cartoon are stupid, and therefore clearly male. The young boy licked his brother's piece of gum because he thought that white powder that coats sticks of gum was dirt. Get it?

Frankly, I've never been able to understand why so many corporate managers and directors feel compelled to treat their direct reports like second-class citizens, but this particular Wicked Witch of the forty-eighth floor took that brand of rudeness and disrespect to a new level. In fact, her demeanor was so caustic and her management style was so confrontational that I stopped fretting about the fact that I was going to plummet to my death because I was secretly plotting ways to undermine the limey hellcat and her delusions of power, global domination, and spontaneous emasculation of any man who dared look her in the eye.

from *Danny Evans <dannyevans@commercialreal-estatefancypants.com>*
to *Helga The Unpleasant <htunpleasant@commercialrealestatefancypants.com>*
subject *Workload*

Helga,
Would you like the number for my psychiatrist?
Sincerely,
Danny Evans
Marketing Associate

Riding the Los Angeles mass transit "system" is a lot like putting your pants on over your head. It's confusing and slow and you know there just *has* to be a better way to do this. To get from my home in Orange

County to my job in downtown L.A., I had to be at the train station by 6:40 a.m. to catch a ride to Union Station, where I hopped the Red Line subway to a station across the street from Helga's lair. This may seem like a rather run-of-the-mill commute to folks in New York, Chicago, or San Francisco, but in L.A., where sitting in traffic is as much a part of everyday life as shitty air quality and shitty breast implants, riding trains feels uncomfortably passive and nonparticipatory. There's no one to cut you off without using his blinker, which in turn means there's no one to tailgate or flip off. And it struck me that if I wanted to live somewhere where my fingers and hands sat idle all day, I would have moved to a leper colony in the Yukon Territory.

A frustration was building inside me, and the more I considered it, the more disappointed I became about how I had been lying to myself. For years I called myself a writer. That's how I introduced myself to people at parties. It sounded nice. Sophisticated. But it had become painfully evident that the descriptor was a lie. Yes, I wrote for a living, but the brochures and flyers I created at my job were hardly the trappings of a "real" writer. I needed an outlet. I needed to put pen to paper on a regular basis. I needed to walk the walk of the talk I'd been talking for too many years.

During my ninety-minute train rides, I began to journal about my disease and the discoveries coming to light in my therapy, most notably about my father and the ways in which his youth determined the kind of parent he was to me—and how closely I was follow-ing his example:

I feel kind of weird today. I think part of it might be to-tal fatigue. I realized yesterday that I haven't really slept through the night in about two months, based mostly on the insomnia caused by the medications I'm taking and so far the inability of the sleep aid pre-scribed to do much more than put me to sleep for two or three hours. I wake up at 2 or 3 in the morning and toss and turn until I just can't take it anymore and I crawl out to the computer. I'm so tired, and I keep no-ticing these odd kinds of momentary dips into a de-pression-type weirdness in my head. I thought by now I'd be more stable and more comfortable with my own brain. But the weird feelings linger and that inspires panic and anxiety in me.

I noticed yesterday that my anxiety is more than just mild and passing, and that it actually is some-thing I've dealt with for my entire adult life. When I'm at the gym, I always reach to my bag first thing to see if my wallet is still there. Where would it have gone? Why do I feel this constant need to check for my keys and my wallet and locked doors and cleared burners on the stove. Why do I feel the need to make sure nothing has been stolen or nothing is exposed to dan-ger? It's like OCD. It must come back to the risk issue and environmental control. Gotta make sure every-thing is where I left it, everything is how I want it. I think this is something I need to continue to examine in therapy. It seems like a variation on anxiety and I don't know that the medication I'm taking is really helping all that much in this category. In general, while I am scared to forfeit the occasional good feelings I am having, I wonder if I'm really getting max benefit from the drug I'm taking.

TWENTY-FIVE

In 1966, four years before I was born, my mom gave birth to a son. His name was Isaac.

My big brother was born a month prematurely, a fact that portended far more ominous medical complications than would be the case now. Specifically, Isaac was born before he developed pulmonary surfactant, a slippery substance in the lungs that helps babies breathe properly. In his case, the absence of surfactant caused Isaac's little lungs to stick together and collapse when he exhaled.

On the second day of his life, Isaac was near death. My dad called his mother to tell her that her first grandchild, her son's son, was not going to survive much longer.

"If you want to see him," my dad wept, "you should come to the hospital right now."

My grandmother told my dad she wouldn't be able to make it. She was busy cleaning the floors.

Isaac died.

In 1998, two years before Noah was born, we had a miscarriage. It was our first pregnancy.

We floated through the first few weeks. *Us! Parents! I wonder what it will be! Will it inherit my two webbed toes?* For some odd reason, we established a rule that we'd keep the news to ourselves, at least until the end of the first trimester. Just in case. But only days later the folly of that plan became unbearable. Some news is too spectacular to keep private, too wonderful not to shout from the rooftops. Our parents cried, then glowed, then jockeyed for position in the delivery room. Our brothers and sisters were overjoyed. Close friends asked for dibs on hosting the baby shower and recommended names so apocalyptic that I wouldn't even have bestowed one on a bowel movement. But had I ever been that happy? I was going to be a dad!

Twelve weeks into this bliss we went to see the obstetrician, an affable guy with more hair in his ears than I had on my entire body. It was a miracle he could hear his patients talking to him through the graying nests leaning forth from the sides of his head like unkempt ponytails. I expected to be a little freaked out by any man who fondles vaginas and their spawn for a living, but Dr. Kingsley made it clear in word and deed that he'd seen more poontang than a Victoria's Secret dressing room. Very low creep factor.

He came in and squirted warm goo all over Sharon's belly (which had theretofore been my job exclusively, but . . . well, that's an entirely different book), and began to rub the magic ultrasound wand over the goo. Thirty seconds into the examination he stopped the wand and squinted at the monitor. The cheerful expression fell from his face like the bikini fell from the hula girl on the pen my friend brought back from Oahu for me. He pushed a button on the machine, then excused himself for a moment. Sharon and I looked at each other blankly, each of us knowing this portended awful things but neither of us wanting to give it credence. I can't recall how long we sat there—three minutes maybe—but time has never moved so slowly. Finally a woman came into the room and walked us ten steps to Dr. Kingsley's office. He closed the door and asked us to have a seat.

He produced a picture from the ultrasound. There was a large black void in the center, and resting at the bottom of the circle was a tiny white imperfection about the size of a peanut M&M. That was our baby. It was dead.

Until that moment I still retained that blind, youthful air of invincibility. I believed anything I put my mind to was within reach, that I was never in harm's way because I was smarter than harm. But that died with our baby. A day or two later, I drove Sharon to the outpatient surgery center so the doctors could remove our baby from her body. (We were given the option to let it pass naturally, but the prospect was far too gruesome to consider.) They wheeled her in and I was left there, alone, while my wife and dead embryo were being separated from one another. I was destroyed. I stood in the cold, windblown parking structure and wept, watching my tears fall over the side of the railing and plummet three stories to the ground.

Although the incessant tears blurred my eyesight, I could see clearly enough to dial a number on my cell phone. I needed to talk to someone I could trust, someone who would dutifully let me weep into the phone. I didn't want someone who would try to distract me from feeling this hurt or someone who would say something stupid, like "It is what it is" or "God has a plan." But who was that person? I was having trouble thinking clearly, and I drunkenly stumbled through my mental Rolodex in search of something I would only know when I thought of it.

I called my dad.

I could barely speak, but he knew where I was and what was happening when I called. I could hear his heart breaking for me.

"Aw, Danny," he said, his voice quivering. "I know how you feel. I've been there. I know it hurts like no other pain you've felt, but it *will* get better. You have to believe that. It will get better."

There was a pause. I think he may have been crying.

"I love you, son."

The moment was far too heavy, but I realized later that this was the first time my dad and I had ever genuinely connected on common emotional and spiritual ground. Mine was a pain he knew intimately. We were no longer just father and son; we were men who'd both experienced the loss of a child.

"I love you, too, dad."

By early 2003 Sharon was beginning to "show" with our second baby and I was beginning to "show" my unmitigated distaste for my job. The personality conflict with my boss was such that I couldn't find a way to work around it, as I had done with my previous asshole supervisors (this is not to say that they supervised my asshole but that they were my supervisors and they behaved like assholes). In the past I'd thrown myself into the work, or at least attempted to, so as not to allow myself time to sit and stew in my anger. But that was not possible with Swiss Lozenge Boss because I had almost nothing to do. Despite my ability and desire to be more deeply involved in the company's marketing efforts, she seemed content to let me do as much as was warranted by my title—"marketing associate"— and nothing more. No trick or sneak attack or opportunistic attempt to stretch my creative muscle could make it past her repellant, so most of the time I sat at my desk, surfed the Web, and tried to find new ways to articulate what a bitch she was. But mostly I thought about my son, my wife, and the new life we would soon welcome.

Anxious, irrational thoughts crept into my head again. What if there's an emergency? What if Sharon goes into premature labor or if something goes wrong with the baby? I'm fucked. I'm dozens of miles away, without a car. Who will help her? Who will save her life? What if another attack happens right here in downtown L.A.? What if something happens to *me*? I knew these were ridiculous, doomsday scenarios. I knew it was my brain trying to mess with me. But given my feelings about the job that was keeping me all this way from my budding family, I seized the anxiety and used it as motivation to extract myself from this meaningless job life. I was sure I could find something just as meaningless closer to home.

Without much effort at all, I found an opening for a senior-level proposal writer at a Fortune 100 HMO in my own area code. After five interviews ("Hi, it's Danny. I'm going to be out again today. I'm having . . . uh . . . *man* problems"), I was informed that I had sufficiently snowballed the appropriate people and I was hired.

"**Y**ou need to be locked in a room with padded walls."

To this day, that's what my mother playfully tells me when something I say or do strikes her as silly. The padded walls are a clear reference to a mental institution, which I find uproariously ironic, because although I've never seen the inside of an inpatient mental health facility, I've worked in more than my fair share of corporate American cubicles, most of which are comprised of three and a half walls upholstered in drab gray fabric padding.*

After my mug shot was taken and plastered onto a plastic security badge, I was escorted to the elevator by a security guard with a mustache and hyperactive sweat glands. I can't remember her name, but she told me someone would meet me when I got off at the second floor. When the doors reopened, there stood another security guard, and further evidence that the prerequisite qualifications to work security at the company were gender neutrality and, if you have breasts, a seamless intersection between their bottom and the top of your enormous Meister Brau belly. The area at the bottom of this torso-long mass of awkward non-specificity was named "the FUPA" (or fat upper-pussy area) by one of my colleagues.

"Danny?" she inquired.

"Yes. Hi."

"Hi, I'm Karen. Would you like to see where you'll be sitting?"

"Sure," I said.

"Good. Follow me."

She took six steps to our left and stopped. When she turned around, she was smiling.

"Welcome home, Danny," she said, as if she were Ty

---

* Anyone who has occupied such a space will see the irony in the congruence of a psych ward and a cubicle.

Pennington on that interminable product placement blow job masquerading as a charitable home-building TV show. "This is your new home."

I'm a humble man. I don't ask for much. And I know beggars can't be choosers. But I have to believe any reasonable person—especially one with the word "senior" in his job title—would have responded to this unveiling the same way I did. Which was as follows:

"Bullshit."

"I'm sorry?" Karen said.

"You're not serious about this, are you? I'm supposed to sit here?"

She didn't say anything. I took that as a yes.

Our friends in real estate suggest a wise investment for first-time buyers is the smallest house in a great neighborhood, so I imagine they would have spontaneously soiled their BVDs at the sight of this hellhole, the worst cubicle on the skid row of Cubicleville. Its padded walls rose to a height just tall enough for me to rest my balls on. Its proximity to the elevators ensured that my concentration would be broken every forty-five seconds by a *Ding!* And as extra incentive, it was also the permanent residence of a groaning, creaking, sputtering printer shared by four people. Privacy, peace, *and* state-of-the-art technology? Is this heaven?

Still, a fine craftsman never blames his tools, and I wasn't going to let an undesirable workspace stop me from kicking ass in my work. Which was what exactly? Oh, yes, Senior Proposal Analyst, National Accounts.

Ding! Of course! *Ding!* That meant my day-to-day responsibility was to take proposals and analyze them, seniorly. At the end of each project, *Ding!*, I would write a report and in it I would declare that I had seen this document and based on my seniorly analysis I could, in fact, verify that it was a proposal. No doubt. It's a proposal. For shizzle. *Ding!*

Title and job description notwithstanding, it didn't take long to realize that in an organization with forty thousand employees, pretty much everybody is a nobody. (In my case, Senior Nobody.) There were three other people with the same job title as mine and about a dozen nonsenior nobodies, and this small army of nobodies comprised what the company called the Proposal Department. Proposals are a big deal in big business, hence the need to staff an entire department with nobodies specially trained to write, analyze, and print them.

Every day our department received at least one big obnoxious Request for Proposal (RFP), a document written by a high-priced consultant on behalf of a business organization large enough to qualify as a "national account." The premise of the proposals was this: "We are a Fortune 500 enterprise and we are canvassing health care insurance carriers to find the one most willing to put up with our bullshit. Attached is a ninety-eight-page list of questions, most of which are not germane to the aforementioned vendor search, but answer them anyway. Thank you in advance for taking it in the ass on our behalf." Since the majority of RFPs were written by the Big Five consulting firms, the same questions were asked repeatedly, which made my job easier because the department had compiled a database of boilerplate answers to the most frequently asked RFP questions. Therefore, each new proposal was little more than a monotonously rewritten regurgitation of *Medical Necessities Your Health Insurer Won't Cover Because a Few of Our Shareholders Aren't Rich Enough Yet and Frankly We Don't Give a Shit About You or Your Perforated Colon.* Still, every new RFP contained at least two or three doozies that defied the rules of logic, common sense, and human decency. To wit: "If an eighty-seven-year-old Hispanic man with end-stage renal failure leaves Omaha by train at the same time a morbidly obese, thirty-four-year-old phone sex operator departs Reno in a barely streetworthy Cutlass Supreme, in which area code is the Denny's where the old guy will attempt to convince the big un' to have gastric bypass surgery despite the high risk presented by her anemia?"

Our account managers would occasionally identify an especially sensitive question in an RFP, at which point he or she would e-mail no fewer than twenty-five people with a panic-stricken missive about the strategic ramifications of our answer to the question. Standard procedure for events such as this was to call an emergency lunch meeting, which I began to call "cockoffs" because the gatherings amounted to little more than a collection of VPs from various departments sitting around a large conference table, each pounding his chest and trying to out-asshole his peers.

"Thank you all for coming," the first one says. "I have a huge cock."

The VP next to him says, "It's a pleasure to be here, but my cock is certainly bigger than yours. My opinion in matters such as this is therefore extraordinarily valuable."

Finally, the VP in the blue tie takes out his cock and slams it onto the table. "As you can plainly see, ladies and gentlemen, my mammoth cock dwarfs your wee units. I can crush a beer can with it, and you must therefore bow down to my cockular humongousness and understand that I'm far too stacked to share my input on the RFP question at issue."

Meeting adjourned.

TWENTY-SIX

I could tell you very little about what my mother did for a living other than to say it was special. It said so on the door.

She worked in a hospital. She wore a stethoscope around her neck and blue linen scrubs. Sometimes after school I called her to ask if I could have a Pop-Tart or some Milk Duds and the person who answered the phone invariably said, "Good afternoon. Special Procedures." See? Special. But one Saturday at the hospital's open house I discovered a catastrophic gap in my understanding of nursing—and a new definition of "special."

To celebrate its recent remodeling and thank the public for its patience during construction, Lost Pines

Medical Center held an open house. The community at large was invited to walk on the new floor tiles, appreciate the precious paintings of earth-toned nothingness that adorned the hallways, and have a glass of fruit punch. Despite the repeated attempts Debbie and I made to elicit compassion, my mother wouldn't dare let us escape a tailor-made opportunity to show us off and pinch our cheeks in front of her work friends. In fact, we were hardly two steps inside the "Special Procedures" room when my mom cleared her throat to get her friends' attention and introduced us to her colleagues. Speaking *at* me but not really *to* me, my mom reminded me that one of the women, her friend Erlinda, was the nice lady who'd knitted me a sweater for my birthday. I hated that sweater. It was itchy and ugly and it felt like an angry Brillo pad.

While the adults tried to one-up each other with tales of their children's accomplishments, I snuck away from the scrum and set off on a safari around the room. I wanted to see the machines they used to save lives and treat people so "specially." There wasn't much I could identify until I came to a row of glass jars, each housing a different household item: a yellow toothbrush, a Ford for President campaign button, some loose change, a lightbulb, a screwdriver, and so on.

"Mom!" I shouted across the room, straining to be heard over the hum of two dozen fluorescent lightbulbs. "What's all this stuff for?"

The question seemed to catch her unprepared. She looked stone-faced at Erlinda, then at my dad, then at Erlinda again. "Those, Danny, are . . . ahem . . . *objects* we've . . . *extracted* . . . during colonoscopies and sigmoidoscopies."

"What are those?"

"Those are the 'special' procedures."

My dad and Debbie joined me at the jars. We stood there together, looking perplexedly into the glass and trying to translate what my mother had said. I could tell my dad knew what she'd meant.

"Did you understand what Mommy said, Dad?"

"Yeah," he said, resigned to the fact that he was about to destroy my entire perspective on life and human behavior. "These are things Mommy and her friends have pulled out of people's tushies."

And suddenly the term "special procedures" took on a whole new meaning.

Given the retrieved goodies at the hospital and the brutal stabbing I'd survived in junior high, I grew to harbor a general phobia of foreign objects in the presence of human bodies—either inbound or outbound. You can imagine the impact such a deeply rooted aversion might have when one is about to watch the birth of a child. But there I stood in a hospital delivery room, for the second time, experiencing the paralyzing revelation that there actually exists a level of hell even deeper than the one where people shove lightbulbs up their butts.

I'd like to sit down for a beer with the person who first described what happens in the delivery room as "a miracle." Or perhaps we could just skip the beer and get right to the part where I hit him on the head with a frying pan. Do miracles occur during labor and delivery? Yes. Definitely. But those miracles have nothing whatsoever to do with the baby's arrival. The *true* miracle is that more people don't faint or puke or collapse into code red material when they see what goes on in that room.

I'd survived Noah's birth only through the magic of adrenaline and Tums. The sundry biological horrors were greatly overshadowed by the realization that I was about to become someone's dad. But the second time around was vastly different. The novelty of watching the birthing process had evaporated, and all that was left was gruesome, blood-soaked flesh and fluids I could not identify.

By the time Sharon was one hour into labor; she had an epidural needle in her back, an IV needle in her arm, and a large mirror at the base of her hospital bed reflecting back an image of vaginal Armageddon.

There was a nurse standing next to me. "Is this hell?" I asked.

"For you?" she said. "Probably."

I hadn't heard Sharon scream with that much unbridled enthusiasm and conviction since the day she nearly lost her left index finger in a tragic butternut squash accident. She was sweating and moaning like a wounded animal. Obviously, I was intimidated. Nervous. Repulsed. Grace under pressure is not close to the top of Danny's Personal Strengths.

I stationed myself near Sharon's head, stroked her hair gently, and attempted to coach her through the pushing. But what do you say to a woman during childbirth? How do you encourage her to fight through the pain when you can barely keep your own breakfast down? If you're a nerd like me, you say this:

"Come on, honey! Dig!"

Sharon turned her head and looked right at me.

"What did you just say?"

"I said 'dig.'"

"What the hell does 'dig' mean?"

"It's what track coaches tell sprinters when they want them to run faster," I said. "Dig your feet into the track and go. So go . . . give birth!"

(Did you know that even when a woman is in the throes of fierce pain, she can still summon the strength to roll her eyes at the stupid things her husband says? They're amazing creatures, these women.)

"This isn't a track meet," she said. "Find something else to say."

Before I could do so, I became aware of something

abhorrent. Pay attention, expectant dads. Here's something they don't tell guys in childbirth classes (because we'd puke). When a woman is in the late stages of labor, her doctor will encourage her to push, whereupon she will constrict her abdominal muscles and attempt to coerce the baby to hastily exit the birth canal. But like any classy restaurant or transcontinental aircraft, your wife is built with two exit doors—one in front, one in back. When she begins to push, her goal is to have the crowd exit through door number one. But it's best that you know that the crowd is larger than your wife is prepared to handle and the overflow crowd will also bum-rush (literally) door number two. Hole number one will produce a baby. Hole number two will produce, well, number two. And you'll never be able to look at a Play-Doh Fun Factory again.

Sharon was not allowed to start pushing the baby out until her cervix had dilated to a diameter of ten centimeters (which sounded to me like an evil variation on "I told you to go potty before we left, so you'll just have to hold it now"). Unfortunately, the medical industry hadn't yet engineered a means by which to expedite such dilation; the mother has to wait it out. It's not easy waiting. It's not like waiting in line at the DMV or waiting for your fingernail polish to dry before you pick your nose. It's the kind of waiting during which the mother-to-be lies on her back with her legs spread apart like the arms of a child when she says, "I love you *this much!*" It's the kind of waiting where the doctor—the one with eyebrows so hairy and so poorly landscaped that his face looks like two Shih Tzus standing butt to butt—leaves the hospital for a tuna melt because he knows you're not going anywhere with those barbaric hemorrhoids developing around door number two.

After laboring for four hours, Sharon's cervix was deemed soft and loose enough to initiate Operation Get This Fucking Baby Out Before I Kill Everyone in Here With My Bedpan. Finally, she began to push. With each contraction, her face tightened, her eyes focused on a spot on the wall, and she squeezed my hand so hard that I was sure my bones were being turned to powder. "Come on, honey," I said. "You can do it. Keep going. She's almost out."

I actually believed my second attempt at "coaching" was a lot more compelling than the track-and-field gibberish, but as Sharon's pushing approached the three-hour mark, even I was getting a little punchy. I fed her ice chips out of a plastic cup. I tried to keep her mind occupied between contractions, chatting with her about the result of all this hard work. And at some point she just looked toward me, her eyes awash with exhaustion, and asked me matter-of-factly, "Danny, can you please just shut up?"

Like a poorly trained boxer, she led with her head. I made a mental note that we'd have to work on that when she was old enough to box. Nevertheless, when the top of her head began to crown and her dark wet hair came into view, a rush of adrenaline pulsed through my being like an electrical charge. It was never real until then. Cognitive awareness that a baby would be born is nice and all, but that first glimpse of an actual human—*my baby*—is like one's own personal nuclear annihilation. Everything changes. Nothing is the same. She was no longer just a concept or a bulge in Sharon's belly. She was a life.

I was all set to start weeping over what was playing out before me until I heard a long, loud primal scream from my immediate right. As it turns out, having a baby hurts. (Bill Cosby once described the pain of childbirth as the same sensation one might feel if he tried to pull his bottom lip over his head, but I got the feeling Sharon would consider that getting off easy.) Her discomfort created a conundrum. To my right was my wife, the woman I love, the woman who escorted me from Nerdville into Manhood. I was devastated to see her in that condition. But to my left was the crowning head of my second child. Terror on the right, joy on the left. It was like Sophie's Choice. "I cannot choose! I cannot choose!"

Amid the chaos and pushing, Sharon managed to, um, "evict" our daughter far enough into the world that her head, shoulders, and chest came into view. At this point, the baby's hips were wedged at the exit door, stretching Sharon's womanhood to a diameter approximating the jaw of a yawning alligator. I've never seen such schizophrenia—she was desperate for the pain to stop but she couldn't believe what she was seeing in the mirror at her feet.

"Come on, Sharon!" Dr. Eyebrow cheered. "One more big push and the baby's out."

With that she leaned forward, took a deep breath, and bore down with everything she had left (which wasn't much). Just as the doctor promised, our baby was out. I couldn't speak. I just stood there mindlessly stroking Sharon's forehead, looking at my baby girl as they wiped her off. She was ugly as sin but she was beautiful.

"Here," Dr. Eyebrow said, handing me a pair of surgical scissors. "Time to cut the cord."

He turned the baby sideways and held the cord tight to allow a clean cut (a critical assist by the doctor given the fact that my hand was shaking uncontrollably). I sandwiched the cord between the scissor blades and closed them, marveling as I did so at how much the tissue felt like the thick rim of fat on the edge of a steak.

One of the nurses took Julia from Sharon's arms and carried her to an acrylic bassinet across the room. I followed her, camera in hand. While my daughter—I have a *daughter!*—was being weighed, measured, and wiped clean of uterine yuck, I turned and noticed the doctor was still staring into The Artist Formerly Known As Sharon's Va-Jay-Jay. Odd. I thought we were done. I looked closer to make sure he wasn't getting his jollies

and to my horror witnessed the birth of the most hei-
nous and ghastly wrongness known to nerdkind: the
placenta. After it plopped out, this doctor, this *socio-
path*, held it up in the air as if to say, "Behold! I give
you . . . the Nasty!" The placenta looked like someone
had taken the layer of melted cheese from the top of a
pizza and was holding it sauce side out. Common delivery room decorum dictates dads should think it's a
miracle and stuff like that, but when you've been up all
night obsessing about your baby being born with her
eyes on her ass or your wife flatlining during childbirth, there's *nothing* beautiful or miraculous about a
big, translucent bag of blood-soaked mozzarella.

An hour or so later we'd arrived in a standard hospital room in the newborn unit. The gathered family
had gone home with promises to return the following
day. We were alone. We were a family. Noah was very
curious about this strange new creature in our midst,
this flannel-wrapped mass of pink coos and cries. I
hoisted him onto the hospital bed where Sharon was
holding Julia, and he moved in very close to her.

"Who is dat, Mommy?"

"That's your new baby sister, honey," Sharon said in
her sweet motherly tone. "Her name is Julia."

"Could I see her, Mama? Could I see Jew-ee-uh?"

He wanted to hold her. To a two-year-old, "see"
means prod, probe, manipulate, destroy—all things
that should not be done with a newborn human
unless that newborn human is a trained professional
on a closed course. To protect our daughter's life, we

jury-rigged a solution. Noah squirmed into Sharon's lap and then I placed Julia in his arms, which were supported (read: controlled) by Sharon. I stood at the foot of the bed, camera in hand, to record the moment. Through the viewfinder I saw them: my wife, my son, and my daughter. My life. Suddenly the shot went out of focus. There were tears in my eyes.

"Jew-ee-uh!" he commanded, trying to get her attention. "Jew-ee-uh! Did you know that I have a doggie at my house? Her name is Wusty (Rusty). Maybe sometimes you can come over and pway wiff her, okay, Jew-ee-uh?"

Sharon's eyes met mine and I began to weep.

I had been so numb for so long. I had felt nothing for nearly two full years, yet there I was, living the happiest moment of my life. How could I be so blessed? How did this happen? Where has this feeling been?

We all sat there for several minutes, and while my eyes were focused on my family, my mind was somewhere else entirely. I realized that while my spirit and my soul had wandered off into some dark hole for all that time, the world marched on without my knowledge. It was like someone had entered my pitch-black world and hit the lights, and my mind was squinting, stunned by the suddenness of it all but not wanting to miss a single beam of the brilliant light that washed over me. I was awake. Finally!

A nurse stormed in.

"Time to change a diaper," she sang.

I remember this part. I remember the horror.

The substance inside my daughter's diaper was not poop. I remembered seeing a documentary about the space shuttle on the Discovery Channel and Julia's first excrement (like her brother's) reminded me of the epoxy NASA uses to adhere the heat-resistant tiles to the shuttle's exterior. It was jet black, sticky, and infused with the smell of death. That's when I got scared. I was beginning to see a pattern of horror surrounding my children and the myriad fluids they dispatch. But I didn't dare let Sharon know or see my weak backbone. She needed me. Julia did, too.

Since we'd been moved to our postpartum room, Sharon had been complaining about her hemorrhoids. I wasn't surprised. I had a pretty clear view of that region during the delivery, and although I'm not a doctor, it looked to me like a prolapsed rectum. But I'm a "hope for the best" kind of guy, so I went along with Sharon's self-diagnosis.

As night turned to morning, Sharon's pain grew stronger. By one a.m. she was in tears. Perhaps that was what set me off. Or maybe it was just the exhaustion and adrenaline finally catching up with me. Whatever the catalyst, I completely lost my shit (see Shirley MacLaine going off in *Terms of Endearment* when Debra Winger takes too long getting her pain meds). I stormed out into the hallway, right outside the windows of the nursery, and began to yell to whomever would listen.

"CAN'T SOMEBODY HELP MY *WIFE*? CAN'T YOU DO *SOMETHING*? SHE JUST HAD A *BABY*, FOR GOODNESS' SAKE! SHE PUSHED FOR *THREE HOURS*! SHE'S TIRED! SHE HAS REALLY BAD HEMORRHOIDS AND I THINK A PROLAPSED RECTUM, TOO! CAN'T YOU HELP HER? PLEASE! SOMEBODY! HELP MY WIFE'S RECTUM!"

In a matter of seconds a nurse arrived with a security guard and a blue balloon shaped like a donut. She inflated the balloon and showed Sharon how to sit on it so her sore bum would be slightly elevated above the irritant mattress.

The security guard was for me.

TWENTY-SEVEN

Given the upheaval precipitated by the birth of our first child, I was quite surprised how seamlessly we all adjusted to Julia's arrival in our lives. It was by no means easy, especially for Sharon, but the fear of the unknown was absent. We'd been through the rigors of dealing with an infant before, and with the exception of my own need to discover how one properly wipes the tush of a baby girl (front to back or back to front?), we became situated rather quickly. There also was a change in my depression when Julia was a baby. It seemed less intense, less consuming, existing as a persistent jackhammering sound in the background instead of an all-consuming evil. I wasn't healed, but I felt progress.

"So," Susan said at the beginning of a session post-birth, "does anyone have anything they want to talk about tonight?"

I looked at Sharon. She looked at me.

"I do," she said. "I want to talk about Danny's job."

"What about it?" I asked.

"He's been so unhappy there for so long that I th—"

"Talk to him, not me," Susan interrupted.

Sharon turned her body to face me. I didn't move.

"You've been so unhappy there, Danny," she said. "I see that on your face and it makes me feel so terrible for you."

"Well, thanks for saying that," I offered, "but I don't have much choice in the matter. I mean, I'm the bread-winner for this family. I have a job that pays decently and provides benefits. I don't like the job, obviously, but it gives us what we need."

"What about what *you* need?" Susan interjected.

The question felt strangely uncomfortable to me. I had never really considered it.

"Interesting," Susan said. "You have an answer for almost everything, but when you're asked to reflect on your own desires, you go silent."

"Look," I said, trying to shift the spotlight onto someone else, "the most important job in our lives is Sharon's job. I do what I have to in order to support her so she can raise our children. I'll do what I enjoy later, when they're older."

"I got news for ya, kid. There's no guarantee that you *will* get older. I assume you know that the suicide rate among depressed people is quite high, yes?"

"Yes, but I'm n—"

"Let me finish. Just listen for a second."

I sat back in my chair. Susan sniffed out the little tricks I'd tried—the faux pauses, the pretend ignorance—and demanded honesty from me, for my own good. She was an attack dog, and I was better for it. She wanted to know about my childhood, the behavior of my parents, the behavior of the depressed "me," my marriage, my career, my kids, my medications, and exactly, specifically, to the letter, what I planned to do with my life. Where no answers existed, she forced me to come up with them.

"It's time for you to start thinking about what *you* want and what *you* need. Right now. Okay? This is real life, and while it's very nice and commendable that you've made these sacrifices for your family, none of it means a damn thing if all they ever see is a depressed, detached, disengaged husband and father. You're not living your parents' life anymore, Danny. You get to choose for yourself, and you'd be a fool to choose to live like this any longer."

I looked back at Sharon again. Her eyebrows rose high into her forehead, as if to say, "I think she just sunk your battleship, buddy." I couldn't disagree. I hadn't been chewed out like that in years. Although my typical reaction to such a pointed attack would have been to retreat and label the woman a moron (behind her back, of course), I could feel myself getting excited by her brashness. She was doing exactly what I knew I needed to do: she was cutting the crap.

"So let's visit this again," Susan continued. "Tell me one thing you can do *tomorrow* that will make you happier."

"I can find a new job."

"How? Specifically? What action are you going to take?"

"I'll start looking on the company intranet for job openings in other areas of the organization."

"Good. Perfect. Do it."

I smiled.

"What are the specific values, environmental needs, and cultural aspects you'll require of your next employer?"

I bent my bottom lip into a U shape, which is what I do when I'm thinking, and for the first time considered the reality that finding a job was as much about what I wanted as it was about what the employer sought in an employee. Not surprisingly, I had fallen into a pattern of believing that having a good job was about pleasing someone else, someone who wasn't me. Susan's question turned that feeling to dust.

"I just want to go somewhere where people aren't afraid to let their employees do their best work," I said. "I want autonomy. I want trust. I want respect."

I felt silly saying it. It sounded juvenile to me. But as soon as that thought entered my mind, I cast it out. I wanted to be done with the rampant self-criticism.

"What about at home?" she asked.

"What do you mean?"

"What action can you take at home *tomorrow* that will help you reconnect with your family?"

That one was harder to answer. I had forgotten. What does a man do to connect with his family? What's something that will make us smile?

"I can play catch with Noah."

My spirit took flight when I said the words. I remember that. I remember thinking that someday I'll have a son, and we'll play catch. That time had arrived, and the realization was at once thrilling and sad. What have I done? Where have I been? This little boy has been sitting there for almost three years, watching me slump and drudge through each day, each year. And all he really wants is his daddy to love him. Me. Where have I been?

The next day, Noah grabbed his little pleather baseball mitt and a squishy ball. I grabbed a bottle of water and met him in our backyard.

"You want the first sip?" I asked, reaching the bottle out toward him.

He grabbed it, placed his whole mouth around the opening in the bottle, and tilted it back. Most of the water that poured out either backwashed into the bottle or ran down the sides of his face.

"Okay," I said. "You ready, champ?"

"Ready!"

TWENTY-EIGHT

There are strikingly similar characteristics between living with depression and working in corporate America. In each scenario, the world is muted and dull. People seem to bleed into one another. Isolation is the rule, and sometimes that's comforting, like a safe zone, but sometimes it's a horrible, lonely feeling.

Although the word "care" was part of its name, it didn't take long to figure out that the presence of that term in my employer's moniker was for cosmetic purposes only. I had the luxury of two points of view—I was an employee of the company (a mouthpiece for it, as a matter of fact), but I was also a member of the health plan it sold. From that vantage point, I was able to see what was promised and also what was actually delivered. They didn't always match, and that made me feel pretty lousy about my job. I was a professional liar. I was like a politician—saying what needed to be said in order to win. I was slime.

It's hard to describe the way it feels to be a corporate whore, but I was no Pollyanna, either. The company was a business, not a charity operation, and I knew I had to toe the line they wanted me to toe or face the prospect of looking for yet another new job, which appealed to me about as much as using someone else's toothbrush. So I dug in and kept my mouth shut. And here's what I learned (embellished a little) (okay, a lot):

Five Things Your Health Insurance Will Probably Find a Way *Not* to Cover

1. Cancer of the lungs, liver, colon, breast, throat, testicles, ovaries, skin, bladder, renal cells, blood, thyroid, prostate, or any of the other organs you need in order to, you know, live.
2. Organ transplantation. (Sorry, kids, but organs aren't Legos. We can't be swapping them in and out.)
3. Vasectomy. Condoms. Birth control pills. Or the births of all of the kids you'll sire because we didn't help you with the first three things. However, in certain cases we have arranged for an agitated mule to kick our members in

the nuts. This procedure has a 27 percent sterility rate. (For the men, not the mule.)

4. Cosmetic surgery, including (but not limited to) the removal of that funny hump on the top of your nose or that weird brown shit on your shoulder.

5. Anything involving an ambulance (by which you should infer that it will be cheaper and easier in the long term to throw your dying grandmother into a wheelbarrow and cowboy her ass to the hospital, lest a trained professional start a lidocaine drip for which you will be charged an out-of-network cost of $16 million and your right kidney). (Note: Removal of said kidney is also not covered.)

Five Things Your Health Insurance *Will* Probably Find a Way to Cover

1. Removal of the eight-inch, condom-wrapped hothouse cucumber that got stuck up your butt when you "accidentally tripped and fell on it" while messing around with your girlfriend and some expensive tequila.

2. Anything for which you will need large quantities of medication (because we need to meet our quota so the dude from the pharmaceutical company will take us out to the strip clubs again) (maybe even the one where we

got that awesome lap dance from Destiny,
who smells like menthol cigarettes, acrylic
nail glue, and Eau de Wal-Mart perfume)
(and if that doesn't make Corporal Shvantz-
enpenis stand up and salute, well, then,
you're just dead inside).

3. Procedures that allow for easy measurement
of efficacy. That's where we get all of the statistical information we use in our brochures
and proposals. However, if these metrics fail
to meet or exceed the previous quarter's
numbers, round up and add 20 percent.

4. Absolutely every requested procedure, including those listed as no-nos in the first list,
as long as they occur within the forty-eight
hours before that cuckoo Jim Cramer on
CNBC interviews our CEO.

5. Can't think of anything else.

In time, the isolation and monotony of my world
stopped feeling so comfortable. It became burdensome
and restricting, but my response to it was unlike anything I'd felt since becoming depressed. There was
something primal in my gut, something that reminded
me of a scene from a horror movie where an alien just
tears its way out of some poor schmo's belly. It stands
over his dead carcass, all kinds of fluids and slimes
dripping from its body, and unleashes a mean, angry,
menacing wail. I was certain that no such creature

was festering in my own belly (because I'm Jewish and the laws of *kashrut* demand that we not eat anything with monsterlike alien larvae inside), but it was something I had to let out. Sometimes on my way to work I rolled down the windows on my 1999 Honda CR-V, cranked the volume on a Rage Against the Machine CD, and yelled until my throat went raw. I reveled in that release. I imagined my voice to be the sound of my depression, and as my yawp shot out of my driver's-side window and wafted over the hum of traffic on Highway 22, with it went the pain and sadness inside me.

Rage Against the Machine was as critical to my recovery as antidepressants and therapy, and that's shocking to me. With the exceptions of Peter Gabriel's "Biko" (a haunting outcry about the 1977 murder of the South African antiapartheid activist Steve Biko) and a few other songs like it, my music collection was virtually devoid of songs containing radical political and social messages. But this sort of defiant, freedom-fighting anger is the bedrock of Rage's rap metal sound. Tom Morello, the band's guitarist, majored in social studies at Harvard. Singer Zack de la Rocha's distinctive intransigence shines through in Rage's jams about Mumia Abu-Jamal, Leonard Peltier, and the Zapatista movement in Mexico. I don't always agree with the controversial lyrical content in their songs, but the ferocity with which de la Rocha barks it and the grinding, powerful music upon which they are delivered elicited from me a visceral response.

More specifically, Rage Against the Machine put me in touch with my own anger—and that's something no amount of therapy had ever done for me. I was predisposed to fear anger (in myself and in others) because witnessing my father's rage as a young boy was frightening to me. There was a volatility about it that scared me so deeply that I fled even the smallest confrontation. I never liked to be around heated debate or voices raised in conflict. I lived this way into my early thirties when my friend Mike, a rabbi who is married to a rabbi whose father is one of the most prominent rabbis in America, introduced me to Rage Against the Machine (I also credit Mike with my first exposure to the Beastie Boys). In the summer of 1993, Mike and I were roommates. He played for me a song called "Bombtrack," which ends with de la Rocha unleashing a primal roar: "MOTHERFUCKERRRRRRRRR!" I bought the CD the next day.

When I was finally able to get mad about being depressed, I listened to that CD and yelled out loud with it. I was liberating myself little by little. I felt the rage. Rage Against the Machine. Rage Against the Depression. Rage Against the Sexual Side Effects and the Pills and the Beer and the Busted Brain.

"Fuck you! I won't do what you tell me!"

Rage Against the Judaism. Rage Against the Accounting Class and Fresno and the Pain. Rage Against the Meshugenah.

"Fuck you! I won't do what you tell me!"

I imagine the sight of a crazy man in an Eddie

Bauer dress shirt and the quintessential family car of its time bellowing profanities and defiant condemnations must have been quite repulsive to my fellow commuters. Fortunately for those poor souls, I found a second method of release—and this one was far tamer.

I had been writing for money for more than a decade, but during that time I very infrequently used writing as therapy or a tool for self-exploration. For a short period in the summer of 1993, I filled a journal (with Keith Haring art on the cover) with my thoughts about a girl I'd just met. Her name was Sharon. I'd never before felt what I was feeling that summer so I elected to keep a written record of my relationship with the girl. (Good thing, too. I married her three years later.) Given that happy legacy, I decided it was again time to psychoanalyze myself through the written word. At first my journal was little more than a Microsoft Word document whereupon I could spew my own conscious detritus. But shortly thereafter I stumbled onto a Web site called Dooce, and I was immediately smitten by its format. Written by a woman named Heather Armstrong, it appeared to me as an online journal, complete with photos and powerfully written tales of growing up Mormon, escaping that culture, and being fired from her job because she'd referred to her boss negatively on her Web site—rather, her blog. It took two seconds for me to realize that I needed a site like Dooce. I found a service that hosted such blogs free of charge and signed up immediately. In a matter of five minutes I became the author of a site called Human Writes.

The subject matter for my first few entries was rather mundane—road rage, shitty colleagues, baseball. But soon enough I began to write about the real issue in front of me. I never found the nerve to publish them, but the entries about depression were the vehicles by which I could check in with myself, understand what was in my head, and ultimately feel around for what I needed to change in order to improve my mental health.

I have kept the depression at bay for a long while, relegating it to the back burner of my mind as much as possible with the aid of the standard, recommended treatments (and some others that may not be so widely heralded by the mental health community). But it's still at the forefront of my world. I still have the fear that I am somehow broken and beyond repair. I am resisting that self-talk as spiritedly as I can, but these are difficult days.

The depression comes in waves, sometimes by way of side effects from the medication and sometimes in the way it first appeared: with a kind of physical sadness and emotional paralysis I've never believed real. It makes you feel crazy, like you might just freak out at any moment. Every time I tried to get out of bed and live like a normal person, I felt a strange sort of magnetism that drew me back under the covers. I shook. I shifted in the bed over and over. I buried my head in the pillow and prayed that it would go away, that I would wake up and realize this wasn't real. But it was. And I had to endure all. The antidepressants and all of their unpleasant side effects. The therapy. Hiding it from the world, which wouldn't understand and would always hold the stigma in the back of its collective mind when working with me, talking to me or about me. It truly does put my reputation at stake.

I believe I've hid it reasonably well. I've ventured forward through the blurred vision, the foggy mind, the nausea, the insomnia, the fear. Writing helps. Staying occupied seems to make the time pass a little faster and keeps me from sitting here wondering how long it will be before I can feel human again.

TWENTY-NINE

I **found a job opening for a senior copywriter in the** behavioral health division of the same health care organization, and despite the fact that "behavior health" was a term with which I was unfamiliar, I applied for the job immediately. Maybe this is it, I told myself. Maybe this is my ticket out of here.

Turns out "behavioral health" is another antiseptic corporate term put in place to bend the uncomfortable truth. The more precise definition of the conditions administered by this department is "mental health," including depression. The primary job responsibility was writing text for the company's member communications materials. These included newsletters and brochures that seemed in my mind to warrant headlines like:

Sad? Depressed? Well, Cheer the Hell Up, Sourpuss

Ten Simple Tips to Help You Laugh at Your Mentally Ill Coworkers Without Getting Caught

Is Your Diet Making You Depressed? Eight Kinds of Food That Taste Like Dog Shit but Might, Perhaps, Possibly Improve Your Mental Health

I was sufficiently awesome during my interview to garner a job offer and a moderate salary increase. But did I want the job? My wife, the Queen of Practicality, suggested I actually sit down at the dining room table and list the pros and cons of the position, like I'd do if I was debating buying a car or moving to a new city or rescuing a one-eyed Lhasa apso from the pound.

Pro

1. More money
2. New challenge
3. Closer to home
4. "Interesting" subject matter

Con

1. A depressed person writing about depression for other depressed people? How depressing!
2. Potential new boss's reputation as "difficult to work for."

I took the job.
Big mistake.

One of my favorite movie characters of the past decade is Gilbert Huph from *The Incredibles*, the Napoleonic corporate blowhard who relentlessly and heavy-handedly badgers Bob Parr (otherwise known as Mr. Incredible), despite the fact that Huph is so short that he stands at eye level to Parr's thigh. Ultimately, Parr boils over and perpetuates a cartoon cliché that never gets old for me: throwing someone through a wall. God, how I wish I could have done something like that to my own personal Gilbert Huph.

I haven't been educated or trained as a psychologist and I have no right to make sweeping declarations about anyone's mental health, but I've been through enough therapy to know when someone needs to be punched in the face, if only to remind him that he is not, in fact, God. That was Gilbert, a short little shit with a fluffy, unwieldy head full of bright orange hair, a lazy right eye, and a catastrophic lateral lisp. In retrospect I find it quite appropriate that (in my opinion) a mentally ill person was put in charge of marketing for a health plan for mentally ill people.

My job in this division was to write brochure copy for those in the plan who were experiencing a mental illness and/or an addiction. All day I wrote mostly made-up prose advising people on how to cope with depression, anxiety, bipolar disorder, seasonal affective disorder, stress, ADHD, grief, PTSD, borderline personality disorder, schizophrenia, and substance abuse. (It was as pleasant as it sounds.) Gilbert's job was to graffiti everything I wrote with red ink* (except for the stuff he really liked, which he would instead claim as his own, rush to his superiors, and stand by to collect the kudos for himself). Gilbert opined that anything he thought of or created or contributed was a quantum leap for mankind. He seemed to believe the relationships he had with his higher-ups were special, enduring friendships (this, according to some of those higher-ups, was rarely the case). Everything he said or did had to be grandiose and brilliant. He didn't think his shit didn't stink; he thought his shit was a work of art that no one could understand because no one understood art the way he did.

After a few consecutive unproductive days in the early months of my tenure, I felt it wise to inform Gilbert of my struggle with depression. The safety of such a tactic was implicit given the nature of our work. Mental illness was our job, our bread and butter, so what better place to "come out" about my own condition?

---

* Red ink was the thread that bound the entire collection of asshole bosses together. Red, as we know, is the color most frequently associated with fire, blood, rage, power, and wrath. Coincidentally, it's also the color of love. I derived from these factors that my bosses saw in me either unrequited love or anger because they loved what I wrote. If you're ever in a position to critique someone else's creativity, find a pen with light blue ink. Light blue is the color associated with understanding, tranquility, and healing.

"Okay," Gilbert said, his face blank and emotion-less. "Why are you telling me thish?"

"Well, I just thought, I mean, given the last few days and the amount of red ink I've been seeing, I just thought you should know that it's not because I suck or because I don't care. There's something else going on. That's all."

He took another bite of his apple, slurping up the juice as he chomped. He sounded like a dog when he ate. A drop landed on his belly, but he didn't notice it and I didn't feel like telling him. I took his aloofness to what I had said as disrespect.

"I don't really know what to do with that informa-shion," he said, accenting his lisped declaration with a fake chuckle. "Thanksh for telling me, I guessh. Any-thing elshe?"

My dad used to tell me to be careful not to "burn any bridges" when departing someone or something. You'll never know if someday you'll need to go back and ask that person for help or do business with that person, so take the high road. Partially because I hated con-frontation of any kind, I lived my young adulthood by that rule, often biting my tongue and swallowing my rage so as not to tell someone what a cocksucker he was or specifically how far up his butt he could shove the job I was quitting. I felt that way with Gilbert almost every day, and that only exacerbated my depression. I held it all in, stuffed it back down my throat until I could re-lease it somewhere else—in the direction of inconsider-ate drivers on the freeway, my wife, my son, myself.

I made no secret of my disdain for Gilbert and his cataclysmic management style. Neither did my co-workers. We all showed up for work knowing the day would inevitably be pocked with interactions with Gilbert that made us feel debased, undermined, and enraged. In fact, virtually everyone in the building knew of his antics and agreed that working for him was an exercise in endurance and tolerance. Fortunately, the presence of so many licensed clinicians with so many different hypotheses about why Gilbert was such a categorical shithead made for consistent comic relief. We all turned into armchair therapists, often leafing through the DSM-IV (*Diagnostic and Statistical Manual of Mental Disorders*, 4th edition)—the bible of mental health care—to try to locate the cause of Gilbert's behavior. I stumbled upon a condition called Narcissistic Personality Disorder, and even though my psychology education is virtually nil and my right to diagnose is even smaller than that, the convergence of my own depression and my presence in an environment teeming with shrinks gave me what I thought to be the mental health equivalent of "gaydar." Gay and lesbian friends of mine think they can spot another homosexual a mile away. I have, at times, been fairly skilled at knowing Jews when I see them ("Jewdar"). And, in the only stroke of good luck associated with being fucked in the head, I had developed "crazydar." Whenever Gilbert was around, my crazydar started to flash and sound an alarm as though there was an incoming nuke. *Alert! Alert! Narcissistic personality incoming at three-*

niner-zero! Get down! Here, according to the DSM-IV, are the diagnostic criteria for Narcissistic Personality Disorder:

> *A pervasive pattern of grandiosity (in fantasy or behavior), need for admiration, and lack of empathy, beginning in early adulthood and present in a variety of contexts, as indicated by five (or more) of the following:*
>
> *(1) has a grandiose sense of self-importance (e.g., exaggerates achievements and talents, expects to be recognized as superior without commensurate achievements)*
> *(2) is preoccupied with fantasies of unlimited success, power, brilliance, beauty, or ideal love*
> *(3) believes that he or she is "special" and unique and can only be understood by, or should associate with, other special or high-status people (or institutions)*
> *(4) requires excessive admiration*
> *(5) has a sense of entitlement, i.e., unreasonable expectations of especially favorable treatment or automatic compliance with his or her expectations*
> *(6) is interpersonally exploitative, i.e., takes advantage of others to achieve his or her own ends*
> *(7) lacks empathy: is unwilling to recognize or identify with the feelings and needs of others*

(8) *is often envious of others or believes that others are envious of him or her*
(9) *shows arrogant, haughty behaviors or attitudes*

If you're asking my opinion, the answer is yes. All of them. Every single one.

I will cop to the fact that I entered the field of health care with a great deal of naiveté. Yes, we live in a capitalist society. Yes, there is always someone willing to push the boundaries of decency and humanity and respect to a new low if it means he can make a few extra bucks. But I believed the health care of human beings was above all of that. Some things are just too precious and important to be monetized and commercialized and profitized. Or so I believed. I snapped to reality early in my tenure with the health care company. I learned that people can be denied the care they need to survive if some suit in a high-rise thinks it's too financially burdensome to the company, which will in turn look bad to its shareholders, who will in turn put pressure on the company to correct these "frivolous" expenditures, which will in turn cost the aforementioned suit his job. Try this experiment: get yourself gravely ill, try all of the traditional medical treatments in vain, and then discover a new treatment that, while still in its infancy, presents you with your last real hope for survival. Then contact your American health care company and request that they cover the cost for the "experimental" treatment. There's no universal guarantee that you'll be denied, but it would be safe to assume that the likelihood of your being granted such coverage is on par with the likelihood that there will be a check for $50,000 waiting for you when you turn to the next page of this book.

(Dream on.)

I'd worked in advertising for several years before this and I'd become accustomed to the art of writing what I viewed as half-truths and sensationalizing unspectacular nonsense in order to get consumers to buy coffee creamer and computer mice and sundry off-the-shelf products that had little bearing on people's existences. I felt I was being paid to lie and deceive, and I accepted that responsibility because the money was good and my clients liked my lies and deceptions. That carefree, caution-to-the-wind frivolity disintegrated when the product being sold was health—and in some cases, life. Whether this change in attitude was a function of guilt or human decency or empathy because of my own need for care, I can't say. Probably all three.

The task before me was to write to people like myself. The depressed. The anxious. The addicted. The beaten. The sick. The hopeless.

Imagine the opportunity: I, a man who had spent the last couple of years trying to repel his own mental illness, was given a direct line to thousands of people confronting very similar challenges. I had so much to tell them! I had so many suggestions about how to tackle the disease—and how *not* to (see 5-HTP). But alas, I wasn't given that kind of license. I felt my job was not to be completely honest, free from the constraints of product placement and ulterior motivation. Rather, I believed my task was repackaging long-standing clinical boilerplate to make it sound like exciting new information. Talk about depressing.

In the run-up to my annual performance review, I was e-mailed a self-evaluation form. This is somewhat common in corporate America, although it has always seemed to me an exercise in inefficiency. I'd never known a boss to actually give credence to my self-eval; they believe their opinions of my performance are far more accurate and valuable than my own. Therefore, before I completed the form with the standard, moderately realistic answers, I took the liberty of providing the real answers.

KEY ACCOMPLISHMENTS—List your key accomplishments during the review year and the business impact.

> 1. *The inordinate amount of time I have spent perusing the Internet on company time has served to streamline the efforts of my internal constituents because they have been spared the duty of correcting, approving, editing, or requesting complete rewrites on work I would have done were I not reviewing sports sites and Googling the names of hot celebrities I want to see naked. Business impact: I estimate that eliminating the need for my col-*

leagues to collaborate with me on actual work
has saved the company $422,000.

2. I have purchased one can of Diet Coke from
the vending machine each business day for
the past nine months, at a cost of 60¢ per can.
Sixty cents times five days a week times four
weeks a month times nine months equals
$108. Business impact: $108. Duh.

3. On a Tuesday in early July, despite my efforts
to the contrary, I actually did spend almost
one full hour working. Then I took a three-hour
lunch because I was all kinds of burned out
from working so hard. Business impact:
$98,000.

4. I sat through the entire Sales & Marketing
meeting without falling asleep. Business impact: I was so tired from having endured that
nonsense with eyes wide open that I couldn't
even surf the Web the next day. That in-
creased the company's available bandwidth,
which I estimate precipitated a savings of ap-
proximately $737,000.

5. I wrote the shit out of an e-mail telling my coworkers that I was going to be out of the office
on my birthday and that they should call this
other chick if they needed anything that I
might normally deliver, which isn't much—
probably just fart jokes and disgusting stories
about what goes on in the men's room.

Business impact: *Since my e-mail eliminated the possibility of rampant confusion and workplace chaos, I'll say I saved the company about $3.2 million, give or take.*

CHALLENGES OR AREAS FOR IMPROVEMENT—

List your biggest challenges or areas where outcomes could have been better during the review year.

1. *When I'm sitting at my cubicle picking my nose, I should probably try to remember to flick the boogers into the trash can rather than discarding them on the floor or wiping them under my desk.*
2. *I could definitely improve the response time of my mouse finger when I hear footsteps coming down the hall toward my cubicle. If I don't speed it up, I might get caught with naked chicks on my computer screen, and I think I read something in the employee handbook about that being bad.*
3. *I need to improve my ability to react professionally when an undesirable assignment is handed down to me. I have been advised that "Fuck that! Why can't Phil do it?" is not an acceptable response.*

THIRTY

Susan could read more than just my words and facial expressions; even something as mundane as a deep breath was evidence to her that something wasn't quite right. Her perceptiveness was impressive, but there were times when I really didn't want to be "found out." I would have preferred to fly under the radar, to wallow in my own self-pity, because it was just a whole lot easier than cracking open my skull and figuring things out for myself. I knew Susan was sharp enough that she'd already decoded exactly what was wrong with me, and I sometimes wished that she would just tell me the answer. I wanted her to save me the trouble of jumping through all of these goddamned emotional hoops. I knew logically that I had to decipher my issues for myself if I was going to make permanent, positive changes to my life, but there were many times when I became frustrated by the duplication of efforts—and I apparently didn't hide it well. We were talking about my job one afternoon and I exhaled deeply. My frustration was obvious.

"Wow, that's a pretty big sigh," Susan said. "Where did that come from?"

"I'm having trouble with this, Susan," I said. "We've talked so much about my work and my career, and I think we've made good progress on that front. But when I sit here and try to imagine what my life will look like in five or ten years, I can't see things being much different from the status quo."

"And why is that?"

I adjusted my legs, crossing my right over my left, leaned my head back, and looked to the ceiling. "Look at the way things are set up for Sharon and me. We made an agreement that she would stay home with the kids until they're both in elementary school, which puts me in charge of our entire income. I have to work, but the work I do is totally unfulfilling and hollow to me. I can't quit, and I don't think I'll have much luck finding another job that pays as well or has the kind of benefits I have now. I'm stuck, and I wonder if this is all there is. If this is the way things will be for the rest of my life."

"Tell me this," Susan said. "What would be your ideal job? If money wasn't an issue, what would you do?"

"I'd be a writer."

"You're already a writer."

"No, I mean a *real* writer. I'd write books and magazine articles."

"But you've already had some stories published in magazines, right?" she asked.

"A few, yes."

"Did you have a day job when you wrote those articles?"

"Well, yeah, but . . ."

"Hold it!" she said. "Don't do that. Just answer my question."

I folded my hands in my lap—a clear display of my compliance. "Yes."

"So what's stopping you from doing that again now? Yes, you have a job that you dislike. And, no, you can't just up and quit because you have a commitment to your family. But is there any reason why you can't start building your next career after hours?"

"Well, for starters, I have two little kids. By the time we get them to bed, it's easily nine o'clock. And then—"

"Don't try to bullshit me, Danny," she said. (Susan was brash, but never *that* brash.)

"I'm not," I said defensively.

"You are. If you really want to make a living as a 'real' writer, you will find the time to make it happen. It does no one any good to dwell on the obligations or perceived roadblocks that stand between you and your happiness. You just have to commit to it, and if you want it bad enough, you will. The only thing in your way is your own self-talk, your own belief that you're not good enough to get over the obstacles."

One of my favorite things about therapy is how frequently what seem to be enormous problems without a solution often boil down to something simple and obvious. That was certainly true in this case, and I needed Susan's blunt confrontation to prove it. There was something more for me than a cubicle and another in a long line of asshole bosses. All I needed to do was decide to make it happen. What a life-changing realization!

When I got back to my office after my appointment with Susan, I tapped out the following joyful journal entry (on company time):

This isn't all there is. The door to that important discovery flew wide open this morning in my meeting with Susan. The model of my father is the safe, low-risk approach. Steady desk job. Don't rock the boat. Grab the lowest hanging fruit so you're sure to get a piece. I have been following this path for 34 years. Don't even think of pursuing the option most appealing to you. It's not safe. Don't try to venture off the beaten path. It might be dangerous. This is such a colossally important discovery for me. I sit here looking at these gray walls, this boring work, this uninspiring bullshit, and now I can tell myself that I don't have to do this for the rest of my life. I CAN build a satisfying career. I CAN do what I've always wanted to do. I CAN deviate wildly from the beaten path and find my own way. This ISN'T all there is.

I'm starting to see with absolute clarity that my incessant search for attention and approval played a critical role in putting me in my current, depressed situation. I have always, always, always assumed that the true measure of my worth is how well I stayed in line and did what I was told. So since I believed these things would garner me approval, I behaved like the little soldier and followed orders, no matter how miserable they made me. True North in my life would be found at the very end of the path of least resistance. It's still like that. I can't make a move if there's risk involved. Do I have everyone's permission? Is everyone okay with this? Why don't you be the one who tells me what to do and what's okay. Wouldn't want to have to fight. Wouldn't want to have conflict with anyone.

I don't want Noah to grow up seeing an unavailable father, a father who is too busy toeing somebody else's line to give him time and attention and an opportunity to speak his mind. Noah will have his own goals; he doesn't need mine. Noah will set his own path, and it's my job to instill in him the confidence to resist when necessary. In essence, continuing to father these kids like I have is damning them to the same fate I have to now undo—looking at gray cubicle walls, sitting under fluorescent lights while the rest of the world is out there moving, doing, living. I wouldn't wish this on him.

This is exhilarating. Transitioning from cubicle job to cubicle job for all of these years has been my way of staying within the lines; the scenery changes, but the job doesn't. Do the right thing, Danny. Support your family. Steady, normal, average-paying job with good benefits and lots of opportunities to kiss ass and seek approval. I'm so thirsty for acceptance and attention that I have sabotaged my own real life's goal for the sake of it. Better to be accepted than to be happy? No. If I'm happy, Sharon will be happy. Noah and Julia will see happiness in me and they will learn that that's what you have to pursue in life. Happiness, not conformity.

The move here triggered all of this. Another move, another gray wall. Yeah, it's more money, but what do I have to do to earn that increase? I have to sit in this depressing environment and write about subject matter that could bring even the strongest person to his knees. "Hey, honey, my day was great today. I wrote about people who are misdiagnosed by their therapists and kill themselves as a result. Isn't that awesome?"

THIRTY-ONE

Going nuts the way I did—the way 6 million American men do every year—clearly does take balls, but the balls need not necessarily be in full, proper working order. You can have the balls to go nuts even if you're shooting round after round of blanks. So despite the repetitive warnings by therapists and psychiatrists and Web sites that I should not make critical, life-altering decisions while I was depressed, I had reached a point in my recovery where I felt I could reclaim at least a share of my autonomy and cognitive control of my brain. Sharon and I talked extensively about the status of our family and the potential of having a third child. But something about one boy and one girl felt comfortable to us, and we felt strongly enough about our familial completeness that closing the baby-batter factory permanently was a wise choice.

If you really want to measure your mental improvement after a depressive episode, have elective surgery—on your genitals, if applicable. The experience is by no means pleasant—how is it that we can build robotic rovers that land on the surface of Mars but we can't invent some kind of sterility pill for men?—but the outcome was a great sign. I survived. I laughed about it. And given that I hadn't laughed about much of anything in almost two years, the humor could be looked upon in only one way: I was getting better.

On the day of my vasectomy, a short, heavyset Hispanic woman in white butterfly-pocked scrubs escorted me to the Room Where Testicles Go to Die. It was a standard medical examination room with the addition of two bone-chilling props: a surgical tray draped in blue cloth and loaded with sharp, shiny metal instruments, and an archaic-looking machine in the corner. (My first thought when I saw it was a recollection of an old Monty Python hospital skit in which John Cleese plays an absurdly hilarious obstetrician who requests that the attending nurse go and fetch "the machine that goes *fing!*") Two wires sprouted from the doctor's machine, and as I tracked them with my eye I found that they led to a small metal plate resting on the examination table. In the middle of the tray was a dollop of K-Y Jelly so mountainous that I wondered if I had mistakenly been led to the Room Where Anal Virginity Goes to Die.

"Get undressed below your waist, climb up on the table, and put your right butt cheek on this metal plate," the woman said. "The doctor will be with you in a moment."

I looked at her, asking with my eyes if she was serious about me sitting in the lube. She shot back a resigned, frustrated glare that seemed to say, "Don't ask me, man. I'm just a nurse's assistant. Just drop your drawers and stick your ass in the goo, okay? Please? Just stick you ass in the goo."

Fifteen minutes later, Dr. Greenberg entered the room looking far too chipper about the morbid half hour ahead. We exchanged pleasantries (you'll never feel like a man until you are alone in a room with another man, you have no pants on, you have one cheek in a puddle of sexual lubricant, the other quivering on that crunchy paper they drape over examination tables, and you're talking college football with the doctor who's about to take a scalpel to your manhood), and then Dr. G. sprang into action. He rolled a heat lamp on wheels toward the table, focused its bright orange beam onto my crotch, and peeled the paper blanket back to expose my freshly shorn ball bag.

"Nice touch," I said. "I feel like a Quarter Pounder with Cheese."

Unamused, Dr. G. described that he'd be using a needle-less anesthesia, which he claimed hurts less than the needle but is just as effective. As he spoke, he began to pinch and squeeze and flick my scrotum with the ferocity of a hormone-crazed schoolboy watching

Pamela Anderson and her implants running and bouncing down the beach during the opening credits of *Baywatch*.

"I'm looking for your vas deferens," he said.

He'd apparently found them because what followed was the first excruciatingly painful blast of needle-less anesthesia—a sharp, direct hit on the lower left hemisphere of my scrotum. The pain caused my toes to curl and I immediately began to feel light-headed and woozy. He repeated the procedure seven times (I counted) and by the time I was numb I was at DEF-CON 3 on the nausea scale. I burped. I covered my eyes with my hands. I went to my happy place (which, given the situation and the shots to my balls, could have been the backstreets of Fallujah for all I cared).

Dr. Greenberg slapped and punched my nuts a few times to confirm the effectiveness of his torture. Satisfied, he continued. I was still trying really hard not to puke and was not at all interested in looking down, so all I felt was tugging and pressure. And anger. And humiliation. And *Okay! It's numb!*

I breathed. I tried to think about nice things, things that make me feel happy, like hockey. And boobies. And boobies playing hockey. Boobies playing hockey in a domed arena that looks like a boobie from the outside. But I was yanked from my euphoric daydream by the low, monotonous hum of a motor followed by the sizzling sound of a raw steak being placed onto a hot barbecue grill. I didn't allow myself to form a hypothesis about the source of that sound, but a moment later the aroma of overcooked mac-and-cheese wafted into my nose.

"[Sniff. Sniff, sniff.] Must be lunchtime," I said. "Smells like someone's microwaving a Lean Cuisine or some Hot Pockets."

"No," Dr. Greenberg said. "What you smell is me burning closed the openings in your vas deferens."

"Oh. Okay."

More tugging. More pressure. More boobies. More smoke. And then, after roughly ten minutes of hell, Dr. G. declared the procedure a success. He advised me to sit up slowly, scoot myself off of the table, get dressed, and meet him at the nurse's station. I said okay. He peeled off his rubber gloves, walked over to a small sink on the other side of the Room Where Testicles Go to Die, washed his hands, and left the room. I found that to be quite anticlimactic, almost rude. It seemed to me that such a significant moment in my life warranted a little more ceremony. Maybe a commemorative plaque or a death certificate for my balls. But no. Nothing. Not even a bag of frozen peas.

I did as I was told, stopping at the edge of the table to wipe the K-Y from my butt with the blue paper blanket. Standing up was something of a challenge for me, very much like the time I took a Nike cleat to the cojones during an Eager Beavers game. When you stand after that sort of trauma has been wreaked on that area, you must take extra care to ensure that there are no sudden movements, especially lateral movements. Worst-case scenario would be to have a collision between scrotum and inner thigh, at which point you might as well just crumble into the fetal position and cry. Fortunately, I avoided any such tragedy as I methodically slid myself down to terra firma. Just as I turned my head to find my clothes, I saw the surgical tray in my peripheral vision—and on it I saw two small pieces of overcooked macaroni coated in marinara sauce.

No, wait. Those are my vas deferens.

"Hockeyboobieshockeyboobies," I said, this time out loud. The room spun like a carnival ride and DEF-CON 3 became smaller and smaller in the rearview mirror. My whole existence weakened and I was forced to sit back down in the K-Y. "Hockey! Boobies! HOCKEYBOOBIEEEEEEEEEEES!"

The heavyset Hispanic woman knocked twice and cracked the door open before I could tell her to come in. "Is everything okay?"

"Fine," I said. "No problem. Just getting dressed."

Ten minutes later I emerged from the Room Where Testicles Go to Die and waddled out to the nurse's station. Through the glass, I saw Sharon and forced a smile. She threw me a surprised look that said, "Holy shit, Danny! You're as white as an Eskimo's ass." I gave her a look back that I intended to communicate, "You have no idea how close I came to puking up that PB&J sandwich you made me before we left. Seriously. That thing was crowning at my uvula."

I grabbed my prescription for Vicodin and walked gingerly toward the door.

———

Three weeks later I have come to the lab. There are thirteen people in the waiting room. As I enter, every last one of them looks at me, notices my brown paper bag, wonders perhaps if I have brought snacks.

Sorry. No. This is my semen sample.

The room is silent, musty, magazines strewn every-where. The mood is identifiably unpleasant (as one might expect from a crowd of people waiting to be stuck with needles). I approach the reception desk, where a rudimentary sign tells me to sign in. The fact that the word "please" has been highlighted in yellow highlighter pen so vigorously that the paper has be-gun to disintegrate under all of that fluorescent yellow ink leads me to believe they're serious.

I set my brown bag down on the white counter, re-vealing a sweat stain on the rolled-up section I've used as a handle, and I begin to scribble in the usual demo-graphic data. Name, D. Evans. Insurance carrier, the Big Blue One. New address since last visit, no. Do you have a sample to drop off, yes.

Before I can even set the pen down, a woman be-hind the counter addresses me.

"Are you dropping off a sample, sir?" she says in a voice that loudly and horrifically approximates the com-bined delicate, dulcet tones of Carol Channing, David Lee Roth, and a goat with a very productive chest cold.

"Yes," I say meekly, holding up my brown bag. "Right here."

"What kind of sample is it?" she asks matter-of-factly, as if she expects me to blurt out the answer, which would imply that saying "semen" in a room full of strangers is, in her mind, no different than saying "sponge cake" or "sign in."

I got the sense that everyone in the waiting room leaned in a bit to hear my response (because when you're waiting with utter dread to have blood drawn by a steamroller of a phlebotomist, there's no better way to pass the time than by listening to strangers use embarrassing words like "fecal" or "urine").

"What are my options?" I say with a smirk, half joking and half hoping that she'll actually run down a list of sample types so when she gets to "semen" I can say, "Yes! That one! That last thing you said!"

She looks at me. I can see her calculating. I am clearly not the first pussy she has encountered in this line of work.

"Is it a semen sample?" she yells.

"Yes. Yes it is."

"Postvasectomy?"

"Yes."

She reaches out for the bag and I hand it to her. She tears it open like Christmas fucking morning and grabs the small, clear plastic cup with the green lid. She holds it up near her blind-ass eyes so she can read the label, and suddenly every single person in the waiting room has a clear, unobstructed view of my spunk.

Then she hands it back to me. (Because I wasn't humiliated enough at this point.)

"Need you to write your name on it, hun," she says.

"Oh. Of course."

You know, it's hard enough writing your name on something round (like a cup), but fill that something round with something you really don't want on your hands and do it in front of a roomful of strangers who know that this particular something round contains a batch of your goo, and writing your name on the something round becomes damn near impossible. It's kind of like wiping your ass with the back of your head.

I hand the signed cup back to the Punisher and she finally dismisses me. She says my doctor should have the results in three or four days. I say thank you, then turn and walk away. I keep my head down all the way to the door.

THIRTY-TWO

I attacked my depression in the way the experts recommended—with a combination of antidepressant medication and therapy. But I was surprised to find that my physical symptoms—fatigue, sad moods, lethargy—abated well before I had finished examining myself with Susan. The discoveries I made in our sessions reminded me of the outdoor explorations of my childhood, specifically when I would pick up a brick or cinder block that had rested on the ground for years. The moment I exposed the patch of moist dirt underneath it, little bugs and crickets scurried from the space in all different directions. Therapy was the same. The moment I uncovered something about myself, new issues came out of the darkness and darted every which way around my consciousness. During a par-

ticularly intense discussion about my need for external validation—a session during which Sharon was
also in the room—Susan asked me if I ever receive
feedback on my writing.

"Every day," I said.

"From whom?"

"From the people who read my blog. They write comments and send me e-mail about what I've written, and
a lot of them say very nice things."

"And what do you do with these e-mails?"

"I have a 'Positive Feedback' folder in my e-mail application, and I file them there."

"Do you read them first?" she asked.

"Yeah. Usually."

After each of my answers, Susan quickly, almost
imperceptibly shifted her eyes to Sharon for validation. After my last answer, Susan saw something she
wanted to investigate.

"Sharon, do you have something you'd like to add?"

Sharon looked at me apologetically.

"Sorry," she said, "but I have to call BS on that one.
He reads them, but then he forgets about them."

"Don't tell me," Susan told her. "Tell him."

Sharon turned in her chair and pointed her shoulders right at me. "It's like you don't even want to hear
what those people say to you. Why is that? Why can't
you let yourself believe that what they're saying is
true? Is it that you don't feel worthy?"

"Maybe. Probably. I mean, I don't really know. I try
so hard to win praise and acceptance from other peo-

ple, but when it comes I have no idea what to do with it. I guess if I don't really believe in myself it's hard to believe what other people say about me, too. Why? What *should* I be doing with it?"

"Read it. Feel it. If someone is reaching out to tell you that they like the way you write, that's an accomplishment you should feel proud of."

"Great," I said facetiously. "I've accomplished something. But that e-mail, as nice at it is, doesn't change the fact that I've never achieved any sort of professional or financial happiness. I hate to be so callous, but positive feedback doesn't cover our mortgage or fill my gas tank. It's like someone you've never met walking up to you and saying, 'I love you.' Yes, they're wonderful words to hear, but what does it change? I'm still not where I want to be."

Neither Sharon nor Susan said a word, and the silence that created was excruciating. The moment after I've made a personal declaration of this sort is always difficult for me, mostly because of the very issue in play that day. I crave external validation and fear confrontation, but more powerful than either of those responses is the discomfort of not knowing which one is incoming.

"What I just heard you say is that you can't truly be happy until everything in your life is perfect," Susan said. "Is that a fair assessment?"

"That comes across a little harsher than what I was trying to convey. It's not that I can't be happy. It's just . . . I want more."

Therapists like to talk about aha moments—momentous milestones during therapy wherein a person finally sees the light on a critical issue. This was just such a moment for me. I'd had no concept until this point that I had taken an all-or-nothing posture—that I was ostensibly robbing myself of joy because I saw stopping to smell the roses as useless frivolity. I had a vague, undefined vision of happiness in my head and I told myself I'd know that destination when I got there. But I discovered that afternoon that my destination wasn't what I thought it was.

When I descended into clinical depression, it was like walking into a haunted house. Darkness was the rule, and every few steps another screaming ghoul would suddenly appear, laughing at my fear. I walked with my palms stretched out in front of me, waving back and forth in front of my torso, tactilely scanning my path for walls and beams so I wouldn't walk into them and knock myself out. It was lonely in the haunted house: I was isolated. But the therapy session and my aha moment were the tiny pinhole that let in a beam of sunlight—a signal that the haunting was changing. Weakening.

THIRTY-THREE

When it comes to parenting, Sharon is a bejeweled princess in a flowing white gown and I am a caveman with a unibrow and a whole tuft of shit matted to my ass hair. I suppose I talk a pretty good game, which counts for something in a world where a smooth line of BS can take you a long way, but when I need to apply my mind in any practical scenario—such as trying to explain to my kids why they shouldn't behave like feral little forest creatures who peel bananas with their feet and fling doo-doo at passersby, I generally come out smelling like a wet dog.

It's as though our children conveniently and spontaneously contract some rare, discipline-resistant strain of the brat flu. During one particularly memorable three-month stretch, their behavior skewed heavily toward the obstinate, rude, irritating, and downright-difficult-to-live-with side of the ledger. Naturally, I take my parenting cues from Sharon because she is calmer, more patient, and light-years more creative than I with respect to the kids. She speaks to them on their own level. She sees resistance as an opportunity to teach. She is a very, very good mother. Conversely, as I said earlier, I'm not a smart man. My methods of fatherhood generally fall into one of two disciplines—celebration for a job well done or absolute deconstruction of the child's psyche because he or she did something "bad." There is no happy medium. You either deserve to live another day or die right here, right now, in front of Pinky Dinky Doo and everyone. And although my trigger finger is quite a bit itchier than Sharon's, there have been times when even her superhuman threshold for patience and grace has been crossed by our spawn.

She once called me at work, her voice quivering and her teeth gritted, and said, "I can't do this anymore, Danny. I want to sell them for parts." I believe strongly that this sort of thing is normal. There are volumes and volumes of literature about certain periods in a child's development wherein they are especially prone to behave like complete assholes—but how the parent addresses such behaviors is, to borrow a ridiculous metaphor from the business world, where the rubber meets the road. If the child sees that such behavior will not be tolerated, he will learn to abide by social and behavioral boundaries. If he gets away with it, he will grow up to be an axe murderer. (No pressure, though, moms and dads.) The question then becomes, how do we teach our children to behave in such a way that we won't have to lock them in the basement?

Sharon and I tried virtually everything. We set them in the "penalty box" (our hockey-minded version of the time-out chair). We took away privileges and material possessions. We made sticker charts and marble jars to encourage good behavior. But there is a limit to what mortal beings can conjure, and we found ourselves completely out of ideas—and the children instinctively know that this is the time to strike. This is the time to take off the safeties, take dead aim, and fire. In our case, it happened one night when I was sitting on a couch between the two of them, just chillin', and it struck me that there was one avenue of behavior coaching I hadn't yet explored: intellect. I couldn't recall sitting them down and articulating the concept of crime and punishment, so I decided to give it a try.

"You guys might not know this, but when you misbehave and act like ungrateful little snots, it makes life a lot harder for Mommy and me," I said. "We don't want to have to punish you. We don't want to have to raise our voices or take things away from you. But when you don't do what we ask, we have to let you know that your behavior is unacceptable."

To my complete astonishment, they were paying attention to me. Noah turned his body to face me and was looking me right in the eye. Julia was leaning into my armpit and shaking her head yes or no when I posed questions to her.

"What I would like from you guys is a promise to try a little bit harder to be good listeners," I said. "If you can show us that you're trying to cooperate, trying to behave, trying to help us by doing what we ask of you, I will promise that we will stop getting upset with you and sending you to the penalty box. You might even get some nice surprises if you earn them with your behavior."

"Surprises?" my daughter said with a cute little inflection in her voice. "Like going to Disneyland?"

"Maybe," I said. "Depends on how good you are."

I let them chew on that little carrot for a few seconds, hoping it would somehow trigger compliance.

"Dad?" my son said.

"Yeah, bud?"

"Your breath stinks."

THIRTY-FOUR

Given that I was so busy training for a lifetime of rabbinical purgatory, I never knew what it was like to play organized baseball. I still find that to be a difficult void in my spirit. When Noah was born, I resolved to guide him in the opposite direction. He was going to play baseball whether he liked it or not—because I *needed* him to. For my sake. I was going to live vicariously through him and he was going to comply with my glory hounding even if that took muscle relaxants and a Taser gun. Did he think he was living *his* life? Ha! He was *me*. I was reborn. And I was a lefty!

If you want to know the truth, he didn't need any convincing from me. The boy loved baseball. By the time he was three he could recite the entire starting lineup for the Anaheim Angels (who have since been preposterously renamed the Los Angeles Angels of Anaheim). On his fourth birthday he hit a Wiffle ball all the way across the street. And when he was five, he had finally met the minimum age threshold to play in the local Little League. This coincided with my decision to finally take seriously the "lifestyle" advice of my friends in the mental health community. The relentlessness of their insistence that I get out, interact with others, and expose my recovering mind to the healing power of sunshine finally broke me down, and I decided to volunteer myself as the coach of Noah's T-ball team.

It should be noted that I knew as much about coaching T-ball as I did about the chemical composition of a Twinkie, but according to the league, I was supremely qualified because:

1. I was taller than every child on the team.
2. I was older than every child on the team.
3. I passed the fingerprint test, which meant I was not a sexual predator.
4. I was dumb enough to volunteer.

In the middle of a dinner featuring Sharon's ever-morphing, content-confused specialty (it usually includes chicken, vegetables, and soy sauce, but it is also subject to the influence of tofu, various types of noodles, and once, tragically, some sort of Vietnamese-influenced peanut sauce), the ring of our home telephone saved me from certain death. I picked up the receiver and heard the familiar baritone of the volunteer president of our league—a macho, middle-aged goober who used to coach varsity baseball at a local high school and thought that should earn him the respect of everyone in the community. As I learned a few weeks later, he was also the guy who strode to the microphone during opening ceremonies, all decked out in his official-looking Easton-branded garb, and dithered on for twenty minutes while every player in the league roasted under the hot spring sun. I was given a list of eleven names and a team name: the Yankees. All of the players on the list were six years old. One was female. One was my son. My first official duty as manager of the Yankees was to call every name on the list and introduce myself.

"Hello?"

"Hi there, Missus . . . uh . . . Smith. This is Coach Danny. I'll be managing your son's T-ball team this season. Do I have any reason to fear you?"

"I'm sorry?"

"No, that was just a joke. A little icebreaker."

Silence.

"So! Is your son . . . umm . . . Ryan . . . is Ryan ready for a great season of T-ball?"

I hear the muffled sound of Mrs. Smith covering the phone with her hand. "Ryan! Ryan! *Ryan!*"

"What?"

"You ready for T-ball?"

"Yeah!"

The muffle vanishes. "Yeah, he's ready. But what team are we gonna be because my husband is a Red Sox fan and he told me if they put us on the Yankees he's gonna kill someone."

"Ahem. Well, funny you should say that, Mrs. Smith. We are in fact going to be the Yankees. Would you like me to have Ryan transferred to a different team?"

"Nah! Fuck him. Maybe this will be enough to get his drunk ass off the couch."

"Well, thank you for your time, Mrs. Smith. This has been a pleasure. I'm really looking forw—"

Click.

My not-so-secret secret anxiety was that one of the parents (perhaps the one who sounded like Flo from *Alice*) would ask what qualified me to coach their kid. I decided I'd have to invent some fantastic lie about being drafted out of high school by the Cubs and then blowing out the rotator cuff on my pitching shoulder, which relegated me to coaching little brats like their Timmy.

The commissioner of the Little League warned me there was a 100 percent chance that I'd have "a problem child" on the team and a 99.999 percent chance that the problem child would be *my* child. Sadly, that sounded perfectly realistic. Noah was at a stage in which he wouldn't even listen to me when I asked him not to throw bars of Irish Spring at his little sister's head, so I *seriously* doubted he'd listen when I warned him that if I saw him getting fresh with his glove on the outfield grass one more time I was going to make him wear his little Bob the Builder pajamas to our next practice.

"I don't *care* if it feels good, bud. We are the *Yankees*, and the *Yankees* don't bone their mitts! *Capisce?*"

The direness of our predicament revealed itself at our first practice. Noah had spoiled me. I thought all of the players would come to practice with at least a modicum of understanding of the game, but it was abundantly clear that at least seven of the eleven kids had never exerted more energy than that needed to open a can of Mountain Dew. Ground balls rolled through open legs without so much as a flinch. Dangerously erroneous throws were the rule, sometimes thrown by the gloved hand and occasionally even accompanied by the glove itself. I saw outfield pee-pee dances on par with the great musicals of our time.

Three full practices and two games later, nothing had changed. In fact, we had regressed. Nobody knew what to do. No one knew where to go. And there were so many nonessential distractions that I was motivated to do what I do best: panic. At the next practice I handed each parent a set of rules by which all Yankees were to abide. This is what it said:

Coach Danny's T-Ball Rules

1. *All players must take a leak before the game so they don't have to stand out in left field squeezing* their wieners and doing the pee-pee dance in front of everyone. Show some fucking class.

2. If you ask me if we're winning and I tell you we don't keep score in T-ball because crybaby little kids like you would go ape shit if we lost, that's still going to be the answer the next three times you ask me. If there is a fifth inquiry, I reserve the right to tell you that we lost and it was entirely your fault.

3. After you hit the ball, drop the bat. DROP! Don't throw. When you throw the bat, it ricochets off of the coach's right shin and drills the catcher in the throat. Then the catcher cries because he thinks he's dying and the coach starts hopping around on one leg and the whole thing looks like a Keystone Kops movie.

4. The coach doesn't want to hear about your guinea pig named Jeter and how its poops look like little balls of black Play-Doh, especially when we're in the middle of the second inning and you're up.

5. No, I won't put your straw in your juice box for you.

6. When you are playing in the field and the ball comes to you, you must attempt to retrieve it. Don't just stand there and watch it roll by. If that were the kind of defense I wanted played, I'd put a beer can out there. I have opted instead for you: a human being with two opposable thumbs. Please use them.

7. *I know more than your father. If I tell you to choke up on the bat and he subsequently tells you through the backstop screen to choke down, the correct move is to listen to me. We'll deal with your dipshit old man later.*

8. *Despite the fact that the baseball is resting atop a stationary rubber tee and practically begging you to hit it with your bat, you are occasionally going to swing too low and hit the tee instead of the ball. When that does occur, we're all going to laugh at you. Because you SUCK!*

9. *It's customary for T-ball teams to gather at a pizza joint after a game. While you and your teammates are throwing pepperoni at each other and begging your parents for more quarters to waste in that machine that grabs stuffed animals with a big metal claw (*cough* RIPOFF! *cough*), your coaches will be sequestered in the darkest corner of the restaurant with several pitchers of domestic light beer, regaling one another with tales of your uproarious ineptitude. Don't bother us.*

10. *Sometimes your mom is going to cheer for you after you've done something wrong, and that's not okay. If you strike out, she might say, "Good swing, honey!" If you throw the ball to third base when it was supposed to go to first, she could say, "Good arm, honey!" Your mom is not helping you with these lies. It's no different than if you'd forgotten to wipe your butt and she'd said, "Nice skidmarks, honey!" Tell your mother to keep her* *placatory gibberish to herself. We are men (men who can't yet hit a stationary baseball, but men nonetheless). Men don't need to be coddled and babied. Men need open, honest, direct communication. And perhaps a little help with our juice boxes (see rule #5).*

Go Yankees.

There were three or four kids on the team who clearly "got it." They could hit. They could throw. They understood the game. Conversely, there were other players on the team—two in particular—who were entirely oblivious. Their attention spans lasted about as long as it takes for a stick of Juicy Fruit to lose its flavor. I practiced with them how to swing a bat properly at least thirty times before each game, yet when the games started and they were in the batter's box, they flailed and spazzed like kids trying to swat a bee out of midair with a wet noodle.

The rules in our league clearly stated that each player must play at least two innings in the infield— even the boys who still think third base is the pitcher's mound and wear their gloves on the wrong hand. This particular rule was the bane of my existence. When the Little League gods decreed this law, they certainly failed to consider the fact that making some of our less coordinated six-year-olds stand that close to a batted ball is exactly like handing them a square-point shovel and instructing them to bash themselves in the head. There was one player on our team who seemed to have difficulty with even the most rudimentary of tasks, such as remembering that you have to remember to bring a bat to the plate with you when it's your turn to hit. For our purposes here, we'll call this player Woody. One Saturday morning I asked Woody to play third base—in part because it was the position closest to our dugout and therefore the most likely spot on the field from which he could hear us yelling at him to take his glove off of his face and pay attention.

Woody lives in a world you and I have never seen. It is a world where everyone wants him dead. It is a world in which he must kill or be killed (there were more than enough dead bees, bugs, and blades of grass in the outfield to illustrate this fact). It is a world in which words spoken by mortal earthlings, like a baseball coach, for example, elicit the same kind of perplexed, crooked-head response one might expect to see from a dog after it hears a high-pitched whistle. On this particular Saturday morning, two consecutive batters hit sharp line drives toward Woody at third base. After the first, which he neither touched nor even considered touching, he stood there, stunned—the way people in the movies do after they get shot. Woody held that posture for a full thirty seconds, well into the next hitter's at-bat. And at just about the time he reanimated, another line drive went whizzing past his right ear on its way out to left field. This time, instead of freezing like a statue, Woody turned to me in the dugout with a desperate look on his face.

"They're trying to kill me!" he yelled.

"What?" I said, flummoxed.

"The other team is trying to kill me! They just hit the ball right at my head two times in a row!"

"No one's trying to kill you, Woody." I said. "We're just playing baseball. You need to be ready to catch the ball. People call third base 'the hot corner' because the ball comes at you fast when you play there. Get your glove up and try to knock those balls down."

Nothing I said could convince Woody that what had occurred was *not* a carefully orchestrated assassination attempt. On its own merit, Woody's momentary disconnection from reality would have been quite hilarious. But it didn't stand alone. It occurred during the same game when a boy's grandfather shrieked at my assistant coaches and me from the stands, demanding that his grandson's swing was fine and we should therefore "leave him alone" (despite the fact that the boy's hands were stacked upside down and he was holding the bat like a golf club). It occurred during the same game when my own son realized in the second inning that he'd forgotten to put on his belt, which he interpreted to mean he is a horrendous baseball player and generally a failure as a human being. And it occurred during the same game when our second baseman was so hopped up on sugar and organic enthusiasm that he felt the need to make every play on the field, teammates be damned. He ran from right field to home plate to tag a runner out. He ran from left field to first base to attempt another tag-out. And after we'd finally convinced him to throw the ball instead of hand-delivering it, his throw from third base sailed over the first baseman, over the other team's dugout, over the right-field bleachers and into the parking lot of the EZ Lube across the street.

THIRTY-FIVE

took a pill every day, at lunchtime. It was about
the size of an Altoid and its color closely resembled
the teeth of someone who smoked unfiltered Cam-
els for fifty years. I didn't usually let anyone see me take
the pill unless they were my wife or someone dumb
enough to believe me when I said the pill is a vitamin or
a Skittle (from which they could infer that I was "normal" and not, in fact, completely bonkers). This pill kept
me from becoming a blubbering mass of tears and snot
at the mere sight of anything even moderately emotional, like a stop sign. Or yogurt. And it is the pill I took
at lunchtime every day, lest I forget a dose and start
clucking and shitting all over the office like a six-foot,
big-nosed chicken in Dockers by two thirty.

I went to lunch one day with four coworkers to a

burger joint decorated with fake birds and plastic palm fronds and tiki tchotchkes. There were rips in the upholstery, carvings in the tabletop, and the kind of sticky yuckiness on the floor that generated a tearing sound every time one lifted his foot to take a step. It was the kind of place where you're motivated to scarf your lunch in a race against your own mind, because you know eventually you're going to start to wonder what was causing the crunch in your burger.

After we ordered, I reached into my pocket to grab the aforementioned pill, which I intended to deftly sneak into my mouth and wash down with a sip of Diet Coke. But in my attempt to quickly and stealthily jam the pill into my grill, I lost my grip, fumbled, and watched as it dropped to the nasty, disgusting, filthy floor and began to roll around under our table. It made two full revolutions around the table's support pole and ultimately came to rest at the feet of a coworker.

"Fuck!"

I slid down in my seat and tried to reach my foot out far enough to drag the pill back to me, but I couldn't reach. There was no other way to get to it other than asking for help from the other side of the table.

"Um, hey, um, Collin?"

"Yeah, dude?"

"I dropped my pill on the floor. It's right by your foot. Can you reach down and grab it for me?"

Without a word, he bent down, put his head all the way under the table, and tried to reach out for my crazy meds. It was just beyond his reach. As he rearranged his body and positioned himself to grab it, someone asked the Question.

"What kind of pill is that, Danny?"

"It's this, like, um . . . an antibiotic."

"What are you taking it for?"

"I have a . . . um . . . a yeast infection."

It was the first thing I could think of, but as soon as the words left my lips, I realized I had set myself up for disaster. I sat there waiting, looking at the eyes of each coworker to see if they would deduce the fact that yeast infections occur within an orifice that people like me aren't supposed to possess. But as I waited, I remembered that only one other person at the table was married, meaning three of them were without steady poontang and would therefore not know a yeast infection from athlete's foot. Their pathetic failure in relationships was my golden ticket out of having to admit that I might at any moment snap and kill them all.

Collin finally rescued my pill and slid it over to me. I swallowed it without even washing it off first because I really, really, really wanted this moment to end.

"Wait a sec," the Only Other Married Guy at the Table said. "I thought only chicks get yeast infections."

"Pffft!" I spat. "Where did you read that horseshit? Guys get 'em all the time."

"Are you sure, dude?"

"Positive. Think about it. Yeast is used to make bread and bagels and stuff, right? So when a bagel gets old and gross, the yeast gets all tweaked and molded. If you eat anything with tweaked yeast, you get a yeast infection. It's basic medicine, dude. Look it up on WebMD."

"Okay, okay. I believe you," he said. "Relax."

"I *am* relaxed," I said. "Pass the ketchup, unless you think that's something only women can do, too."

Talking about my disease in therapy and with my fellow depressed men had a noticeably positive effect on me. The more we talked, the less alone I felt. The more connected I seemed to be with my peers, the better I felt. And the better I felt, the more attention I could turn to implementing what I had learned and devised with Susan. The stigma still existed, some of the symptoms of depression still lingered for me, but I was a changed person. I stopped actively working to keep my own secret. It was okay with me that people knew I wasn't perfect, and I stopped taking responsibility for the reactions of other people who found out and weren't sure what it meant. That was *their* problem. If knowing that I was recovering from a mental illness meant that they no longer wished to acquaint themselves with me or that I was somehow a diminished human being, fine. I convinced myself that if people were inclined to think that way, it was better for me because I could focus my friendships on the people who stood behind me whether they understood my disease or not.

While that approach worked well in the physical world, I wondered how it would play in the virtual world—on the Internet. As much as we'd all like to believe that people are generally good and decent and respectful, there are far too many online examples to the contrary, and those examples were sufficiently vicious and hateful and generally fucked up to challenge my desire to share my depression story on Human Writes, which I had since renamed Dad Gone Mad. I've seen it proven time and again that the moment you put something on the Internet, even something as innocent as a sweet picture of your child, you lose control over that content forever—and there are destinations online that have risen to prominence and profitability by doctoring that picture and reposting it with a poorly drawn penis on it or labeling the child in the photo a "retard." That sort of immorality happens all the time on the Internet, and it challenges one to post information about his life at his own risk. I mulled that reality for weeks before I "came out" about my mental illness on Dad Gone Mad. I knew whatever I wrote could be turned against me, could influence potential employers, and could be weaponized in ways beyond my imagination.

Ultimately, those very threats were what convinced me to go through with the online revelation. I surmised that vitriol of that sort is powered by ignorance, and that ignorance is what has propelled the stigma associated with mental illness to the point that its sufferers must hide from it. The longer we hide, the bigger the stigma grows. It's the quintessential self-fulfilling prophecy. In the end, I suppose I was just tired of hiding. Aside from a Dukakis rally I attended at UCLA the night before he was thoroughly trounced by Bush Sr., I have never been a particularly cause-oriented person. I've never cared enough about a cause to stand behind it. But because this issue was so personal and so much a part of who I had become, I saw writing about my experience as a small, moderately significant way of driving a stake into the stigma. I removed the veil with an entry entitled "The Devil Inside":

This is the entry I have known was coming for quite some time, but I have dreaded the notion of putting into text the thoughts that follow. I have no concept of what good can possibly come from publishing these words. But I began this site as an outlet for myself, and what I have to say simply needs to come out.

Almost three years ago, I was diagnosed with clinical depression.

I take antidepressant drugs.

I see therapists.

I struggle.

Many, many people—myself included—balk somewhat at the mere mention of depression. It conjures images of weakness and unrealistic vulnerability, of someone who is merely a scintilla short of bona fide psychosis, of someone who is not mentally or emotionally or spiritually strong enough to cope with even the most basic disappointments in life. That, of course, is untrue. But the stigma remains.

For three years, I have done my best to hide my depression from view. I'm embarrassed by it and scared of dropping several notches in the eyes of others who do not understand, or even wish to try. But the incessant game of hide-and-seek becomes exhausting and stressful and only serves to fuel the self-doubt. For three years, whenever I have told people that I have this disease, I have watched as they wonder in a panic what it means. I have kept the depression at bay for a long while, relegating it to the back burner of my mind as much as possible with the aid of the standard, recommended treatments (and some others that may not be so widely heralded by the mental health community). But it has roared to the front of my world during the last five days, once again igniting the fear that I am somehow broken and beyond repair. I am resisting that self-talk as spiritedly as I can, but these are difficult days.

And then there's this: Monday morning, a Dad Gone Mad reader wrote to me and told me that her mother is having brain surgery tomorrow. She said her mom is a huge fan of this site and that if I could send her a quick "good luck" e-mail, it would help a lot during some very frightening days. I obliged, of course, telling her to ask for a bag of frozen peas to put on her scar when she gets to the recovery room.

I don't know that I can even begin to articulate what a request like that means to me or what it does to my soul. How can I wallow? Woe is NOT me. As the old book title says, "Your Blues Ain't Like Mine."

Perspective is a mighty weapon. Yes, I have something to confront. Yes, it's difficult. Yes, I would prefer to ignore it and hope that it goes away. But it won't. And neither will I.

A few moments after I hit "publish" on that entry, readers began to leave comments on what I'd written. I was prepared for this, keenly aware of the propensity for anonymous Internet shitheads to take gratuitous and downright mean shots at bloggers who write anything remotely controversial or revelatory. It comes with the territory, but I was fortunate to have spent enough time as a journalist to know that a thick skin is as critical an instrument for a writer as a pen. (When I was nineteen, I wrote a short feature story about a young Russian girl who'd defied the odds by coming to the United States on a full scholarship from a Jewish summer camp. An editor at a Los Angeles Jewish magazine rejected the submission outright, shrieking, "This isn't journalism! I don't know *what* it is, but it isn't journalism.") Lo and behold, a commenter who declined to state his name wrote, "Oh, shake out of it ppl! it's fashionable to be depressed these day, what with the affluenza. if some of you folks learnt how to give instead of just take take take, then maybe just maybe you'll shake yourselves of this self imposed loneliness and depression that you need happy pills and endless cups of starbucks coffee to treat."

But to my complete amazement, the overwhelming majority of responses to my depression post were utterly devoid of criticism or teasing. One after another, commenters stepped forward to say, "Me, too." One wrote, "I've been sruggling [sic] with depression since the very beginning of high school. And while I'm only 23 and probably among your youngest readers, I completely understand what you are talking about . . . This post made my heart skip a beat, I felt like you were writing about me!"

"I've been battling depression and an anxiety disorder since I was 16," another reader wrote. "I'm 35 and have been on medication only since I turned 32. What did it for me was the day I realized that my 'moods' were affecting my husband and baby daughter. Now I have three kids total (and still have the hubby), and I'm thankful daily I finally began to deal with the illness that hobbled me for so long."

Young and old, men and women, from all over the world, depressed people were stepping out of the shadows to share their own stories of depression and other mental illnesses. Some wrote the names of the medications they took. Others described the specific personal issues they believed caused their depression. And some went so far as to articulate the depression they felt at that very moment. "Some days are good for me and I forget that I ever worry or feel down . . . other days, it gets the best of me and I lose it," a reader named Jacqueline wrote. "Today, I'm on the verge of losing it."

Comments continued to trickle in for several days and I found my personal sense of depression's insidiousness in the world expanding as I read each new comment. Perhaps the attachment of names and sto-

ries to each one changed my perspective. But the one
phenomenon I could not wrap my head around was
the contention by some of the readers that I had performed some sort of heroic act by "coming out" with my
depression. I found it at once thrilling to get that sort
of validation and disconcerting that something so simple could have such an impact on so many people. Said
one commenter, "My appointment for a referral is tomorrow. Consider yourself responsible for my taking
the first step away from the emptiness." It occurred to
me there was something broken—that if just getting
this small sampling of people to *discuss* their mental
illness made them feel this free, how big must this
problem be in the rest of the country? How many of
us are suffering? And who's going to get *them* talking?
I found part of the answer in another comment in
the list, this one left by someone who called herself
FWMama.

"I first came across your blog when my husband began treatment for anxiety/depression," she wrote. "I
was having trouble coping with it. I couldn't understand why he couldn't just snap out of it. In a fit of
boredom, I was thumbing through your old entries,
and found a few that mentioned your struggles with
depression. The way you thanked [Sharon] for her patience was touching. It made me realize that I have to
support the man I love. In sickness and in health, ya
know? And your comments helped me better understand what my husband was/is going through. He

doesn't articulate his feelings well. You gave me some insight on what he was struggling with. Hang in there."

I wondered to myself whether this woman's husband had any notion that his wife was coming to his rescue. I was fortunate beyond measure to have a wife with similar purpose—a woman who found it in herself to help me get up off of the floor even after all she'd endured while I was down. But not all wives and girlfriends could be so selfless, could they? Would they even know depression if they saw it? The dialogue would have to be continued not just for the men who were depressed, but for the people who love them, as well. They needed to know. They needed to have a window through the social stigma so they could see what mental illness looks like, sounds like, and feeds on. They needed to know so they could help us when we need the help.

THIRTY-SIX

The Friday nights of my youth were all the same: the whole family piled into my mom's Camry and headed to dinner at China Palace—a quaint, windowless restaurant at the end of a strip mall near our house. Although my sister and I often dreaded having to spend another night picking the little pieces of spicy red pepper out of our kung pao chicken while all of our friends were out partying, the egg rolls and hot mustard softened the blow. The lobby area of China Palace was pretty cool as family restaurants go. There was a big fish tank and a bar and a small TV that was usually tuned to the Lakers game, which was fine by me because I thought Magic Johnson was god.

The lobby decoration most appealing to my dad was the faux gold statue of a big Chinese dragon and his little dragon pup. More specifically, the papa dragon's left front paw rested on top of the little dragon's head—a representation of the papa dragon's superiority and power.

"You see that big dragon right there?" my dad said with a wry smile. "That's me. And that little baby dragon under his foot? That's you. And don't forget it."

"Psht. Whatever, Dad," I said. And then, without exception, we would engage in a faux wrestling-fighting-slapping match that was always quiet enough not to disturb the other patrons but always loud enough to make my mother hide her face out of sheer mortification.

"Guys!" she'd loudly whisper to my dad through her lingering Chicagoan accent. "Stop thyat."

I've long since moved away from that town, but I'm told China Palace still stands in the same spot at the end of the same strip mall, right next to the donut shop.

One morning, without my knowledge, I became the papa dragon. Noah picked a fight with me. He punched me in the shoulder, ran me down, and punched me again.

"Boy," I said in my best Southern accent, "don't start a fight you can't win. And don't bring a knife to a gun-fight. Y'hear?"

"Psht. Whatever, Dad," he said.

In two seconds flat I had him on the ground, flat on

his back. I sat on top of him and pinned his arms to the ground. As he struggled powerlessly to squirm loose, I smiled at him, taunted him, stuck my tongue out at him. He started to laugh.

While I had his undivided attention, I told him the story about the dragon statue at China Palace. I told him that I'm the papa dragon and he's the baby dragon, but someday, when he's a dad, he can be the papa dragon just like me. He looked at me intently.

"Dad?"

"What, bud?"

"You're sitting on my wiener."

The funny thing about wieners is that when you're raising a son, it seems to be a daily topic of discussion. There are discoveries and explorations and questions about why it looks so unusual. Sometimes such conversations are carefully planned and scripted, like when you're telling the boy why he should not expose it to large groups of people. But there also are occasions when spontaneity requires quick, off-the-cuff thinking.

Having been around sports in one way or another for all of my adult life, I have long since come to terms with the fact that sometimes athletes get hurt. I've seen guys break their legs, blow out their knees, and snap their Achilles tendons. I have personally taken a few basketballs in the nose, sprained my ankles, and overextended myself so far that I've had to stop and lie down in the middle of the playing field so as not to faint. But for most of my life I have taken a rather cavalier attitude about sports injuries. It happens. It's part of the game. It hurts for a few minutes, but you walk it off, rub some dirt on it, squirt some Windex on it, take a deep breath, and get back in the game.

But it's funny how seeing one's own son get drilled in the nuts by a baseball changes one's perspective.

The sun sets behind right field in the late innings on the field where Noah played, meaning batters looked directly into the blinding glare. In the fifth inning of a Wednesday night game, Noah was playing in the pitcher's spot. I was standing near the right-field foul line, failing miserably in my attempt to keep our outfielders focused on the game instead of the shiny black stinkbugs that scurry through the outfield grass. Suddenly, a hit. The ball shot through the gap between first and second base, right into the waiting glove of our right fielder, Nate. The runner was lightning quick (by little kid standards), so Nate made the proper decision to throw the ball in to the pitcher (which in our league meant the play is over and the runners must stay where they are).

The next five seconds passed in super slow motion. Since I was standing about ten feet from Nate, I saw the flight and velocity of his throw from the perfect perspective. I'd been watching Little League baseball for almost a full season by this point, and I'm not sure I've ever seen a more perfect throw. It was right on target to the pitcher, my son, whose body was facing

Nate's incoming throw but whose eyes were blinded by the extraordinary glare of the sun behind Nate. Ready or not, that ball was incoming, but he never saw the ball. *Boof!* Right in the nuts.

My beautiful boy fell to the ground like he'd been shot and curled himself into the fetal position. The coaches from both teams ran to him, as did I. By the time I got there from way out in right field, the coach from the Dodgers (*cough* Asshole! *cough*) had forced my kid to stand up and was pushing him in the back.

"Walk," he was saying. "The best thing to do for this is walk."

Noah was crying, doubled over, hardly able to walk. When I made it to his side, I physically removed the hand of the Dodgers coach from my son's back.

"He has to walk," the coach demanded. "Make him walk."

Had we not been surrounded by young boys, and had my daughter not been crying in the bleachers because she was scared for her brother, and had I not been concerned for my son and his balls and my future grandchildren, I'm fairly certain I would have said something about that guy's mama. As I have said, I don't really care for confrontation—but every man has his limit. Even men recovering from a mental illness.

"I'll take it from here, Coach," I said. "He's my son."

My poor kid. He was hurt and scared and embarrassed to be crying in front of his teammates. I hugged him. I told him he was okay and that I knew it hurt really bad but it would go away in a few minutes. I could see him trying to be brave, trying to will his tear ducts closed, trying to do the things men and boys in our culture instinctively do when they find themselves getting emotional.

"It hurts, Daddy."

"I know, honey. Do you want to go take a seat in the dugout for a little bit?"

He shook his head no. He's a tough, stubborn kid, and I tried to soothe my own nerves by interpreting his determination to play on as a sign that he was going to be all right. I needed that to be true. For me. For him. For his mom and sister.

After about five minutes, he began to wipe the tears from his eyes. His face changed from anguish to determination.

"I'm okay," he said. "Let's go."

"Are you sure?" I asked. "You don't have to be brave."

He shook his head up and down and moved his shoulders and arms so as to wiggle free from my embrace. Then he walked back to his spot on the field and punched the pocket of his baseball glove with his bare fist. Game on.

"I guess that officially makes you a baseball player," I said to him. "You can't be legit until you've taken one in the junk."

He smiled and punched his mitt again.

I felt out of sorts as I trotted back to my position in right field. We seemed to have just crossed a threshold of some sort. When the ball first hit him and I rushed in, he was still a little boy who was scared and hurt. He needed his daddy, and I suppose it was satisfying to me to be needed (in spite of the shitty circumstances). One of fatherhood's greatest gifts is the opportunity to be there to support one's kids, to protect them, to soothe them. To feel needed. To come through for one's kids when they need their daddy. To me, there is no truer representation of "being a man." But something changed when he started to feel better, when he started to realize he was going to be okay. He wanted me to go away. He wanted to shed my embrace, to excuse himself from the protection I was giving him and get on with the game. At some unspecified moment during that five-minute span, he found his independence. He discovered that there are decisions he can make and behaviors he can inhabit on his own, without his daddy shielding him and soothing him and rubbing his back. Here I thought he was still my little kid—the boy who still needed help flossing his teeth, still wanted every toy he sees advertised on TV, still wanted his mom and me to lie on his bed with him for a few minutes before he went to sleep. But that afternoon I saw the porcelain shell that was his little boyhood begin to crack and break, and underneath it was a new boy I wasn't ready to see. I wasn't done being needed by him. I wasn't done holding his hand when we crossed the street. I wasn't ready for what I saw. But I didn't have a choice.

THIRTY-SEVEN

In my mind, the difference between a town and a city is the presence of a shopping mall. Not a strip mall or a so-called mini-mall, mind you, but a bona fide shopping mall with a food court and a Macy's and a colorful little train that choo-choos around the shops during the holidays. Since I moved away from Simi Valley in 1993, I have teased my parents (particularly my mother) about the fact that they still live in the Podunk little town we moved to when I was two years old. A town *without* a shopping mall.

"Daniel," my mom said when she called, "I have some news for you." (She only calls me Daniel if she's mad or indignant.)

"Oh, yeah? What's that, Ma?"

"We're getting a shopping mall," she said. "Put that in your pipe and smoke it, mister."

Sure enough, the Simi Valley Town Center opened for business a few years ago, complete with the requisite food court, Macy's, and colorful little train. Every visit we've made since has included a trip to the mall, and each time we go I marvel at how much the quaint little Simi Valley of my youth has become the City of Simi Valley, population 126,000 (and growing). It has come a long way since Bottle Village.

We were having lunch at the Simi Valley Town Center one sunny Sunday afternoon when out of nowhere the typically surface-level conversation with my dad suddenly went deeper into the well of emotion than any chat we'd had since I called him after our miscarriage. We were eating hamburgers out of red plastic baskets, leaning in to hear one another over the caterwauling of other patrons, and my dad began to tell me about his childhood. There was a distance in his eyes that I didn't recognize.

"I didn't know," he said, his voice trailing off. "All those times . . . I thought it was my fault. I thought I had done something wrong—that maybe I didn't deserve their love."

I'd never seen my dad so vulnerable. He'd turned seventy mere months before then, and with his advancing age came a set of medical challenges that transformed the tall, stoic, dominating patriarch of my youth to a frail, rickety man who walked with a cane and relied on a medicine cabinet full of pain medications to help him traverse each crippling day. Sitting there, listening to my father's torturous recollection that his parents never told him they loved him, I began to understand him. Through him I gained a new understanding of myself, and of the way our respective vulnerabilities have bound us together.

My father's youth in Altoona exposed him to emotional and spiritual torment unlike anything I can fathom. I have no sense of how it feels to be unnoticed or disregarded by one's parents. My dad never knew where he stood, never could forecast with any certainty when he would be summarily moved to another room, another state, another raw emotional place. He was perpetually vulnerable, so it's no wonder that he grew up to become the kind of man who would not allow himself to be in that position ever again. What is the opposite of vulnerable? Hard? Impenetrable? Inaccessible? Yes. This was the father I knew, and because this was the posture he chose to take against the world, I raged against him and became vulnerable myself. I believe that was the root of my depression, and I now know that without his knowledge or intention, my dad passed down to me a sense of powerlessness over my own course in life. Like him, I went where I was told to go. I marched down that path until my mind decided it couldn't take any more and broke down in the fall of 2001. With the hard work of therapy, I found ways to close the holes in my life where the harsh, blinding light of vulnerability could shine through and burn me. I took myself apart like a busted carburetor, examined the pieces, retrofitted where necessary, and rebuilt myself to be stronger—new and improved.

As we sipped Diet Coke and dredged undercooked steak fries through small mounds of ketchup that afternoon at the Simi Valley Town Center, my dad and I reversed our roles. *He* was the one taking himself apart, exploring parts of his memory long since locked away and blocked out. He remembered being banished from his best friend's home by the boy's father because the elder had been insulted by an insensitivity uttered by my grandmother. Memory after memory, hurt after hurt, my dad's shoulders hunched over a little farther. There were lengthy pauses here and there, sometimes midsentence, where I saw him look off into the distance as another painful recollection flooded back to his consciousness.

The kids had finished their meals and were beginning to get restless. It was time to go. The waitress brought our check and I tried resolutely to grab it out of my father's hand (this is a dance we do every time we go out to eat together), but he wouldn't relent. He dropped his credit card into the rectangular vinyl folder in which the bill was delivered and handed it back to her. As she walked away, I looked at my dad's face. His salt-and-pepper hair was beginning to look a lot more salt than pepper, and his face reflected the difficulty of the memories swimming around inside his head. His left hand lay flat on the table, just to my right. As a child I thought my dad's hands were enormous—big, beefy fingers and a palm the size of a salad plate—but as I looked at it at that moment it seemed to be no bigger than *my* hands. It felt equal.

I placed my hand on top of his. He turned his head and looked me in the eyes.

"It wasn't your fault," I said. "Can you see that now?"

He pulled his hand out from under mine, placed it on top, and gently, lovingly squeezed my hand.

THIRTY-EIGHT

If there's one thing I've learned in my first decade of fatherhood, it's this: the guys who talk about it like it's a charming, noble, life-affirming pursuit are morons of the highest order. With all due respect (and that may be very little), the real truth is that being a dad is sometimes an imposition of pain far worse than any up-the-peen catheter could ever deliver. We walk through our wives' pregnancies in some dim-witted prepartum stupor, having convinced ourselves that if we're savvy enough to plunge a toilet or change the spark plugs on a Camry, raising a child is as easy as opening a can of soup. Then comes the day our child is born and all of that cockiness and confidence wilts like a week-old head of romaine.

We're such idiots. We stare into our wife's crotch expecting to see the kid's head but instead we see an enormous human arm jet out and grab us firmly by the throat. The tattoo on the bicep reads "FATHER-HOOD." While it chokes us, it whips our body around the delivery room, smashing us against instrument trays and stirrups and bassinets. It speaks. "You think you can take me, punk? You think you're stronger than me? Well, I've got news for ya. I'm about to put you in a world of hurt! For the next eighteen years I won't let you sleep, I won't give you a moment of privacy, and I won't even let you bang your wife without interrupting the festivities to tell you your kid peed the bed and you need to clean it up. And you know what? You're gonna like it." Then the fist releases its grip and slithers home into your wife's uterus.

That's how it felt to me anyway.

But as my depression gradually subsided and little by little I started to feel like a functional human being again, I rediscovered why I wanted to have children. The fog around my existence slowly burned away and in the clarity I found that my little babies were becoming great kids. They were cute and cuddly. They were real people. They could converse and wrestle and understand my commands. While I was away, distracted by the relentless terror of my disease, Sharon kept nurturing them, teaching them, and doing the work of mother *and* father. And through it all, they never stopped loving me—even during the times when my behavior was unlovable.

This is not to say that my children were model citizens twenty-four hours a day. As much as I would look forward to leaving work so I could get home to see them, there were days when I dreaded opening our front door because I knew that pure hell was waiting on the other side. One night I arrived home after an especially disgusting day at the office and was accosted at the door by two whiny, clingy, catastrophically tired children. They grabbed hold and hung on to me like a wet towel on a hook. When I finally unlatched their superheroic kung fu grasps from my be-Dockered legs, I walked over to kiss my wife. As soon as my lips separated from hers, she said, "Don't forget I'm going out tonight, honey. You'll have the kids to yourself." A smart man would have run for his life. A man with even a shred of inclination toward self-preservation would have negotiated some sort of mutual understanding with his wife—an agreement that a personally offensive requirement such as this would need to be properly "appreciated" upon her return. But I am neither smart nor a particularly strong negotiator. I silently acquiesced because for some stupid reason I felt this crazy obligation to be an active father—even in times when all I wanted was a beer and the remote control—because I just couldn't get past the fact that I love those kids with the white-hot fury of seven thousand suns. And let me tell you, it's a real inconvenience sometimes.

She left. She got into her minivan and drove away, abandoning me there with Marty McWhineypants and

Sally Snottybottom. They *kvetched* all night. *Daddy-iwantsomegrapes. Daddycanyoureadthistome? Daddy-canwehavedessert? Daddydaddydaddy.* And when I sat on the floor and played Legos with them, it wasn't even close to enough. The airplane wasn't big enough. The monkey's leg fell off. The house had no windows. "Fix it, Daddy! Fix it!"

By bathtime I was cooked. I hadn't eaten dinner, hadn't checked my e-mail, hadn't done a thing for my-self. And still: the whining. The first three times I asked them to get undressed, this was their response: "_____."

The fourth time was different. I didn't ask.

"Guys! Listen! I want you to go into your rooms, take your clothes off, and meet me in the bathroom in thirty seconds. Go. Now." My tone was sufficiently intimidat-ing to motivate action—and that was an entirely foreign sensation for me because I have never intimidated any-thing. Forty-five seconds later they were butt-naked, freshly pee-peed, and standing under a running shower (but doing so with a cowering posture that offered the smallest possible chance that they would actually get wet). I left them there for a moment. I needed thirty sec-onds of peace—enough time to throw together a PB&J and fire up my computer. As I spread the Skippy, I be-gan to wonder to myself how stay-at-home parents en-dure this all day. How do they stay sane? How do they find the time to do the things they need to do *for them-selves*? How do they—

Hold it.

It's quiet. Too quiet. It shouldn't be this quiet. This can't be good.

I set down my sandwich and stormed back to the bathroom, all the while girding myself for the carnage I knew I'd see when I got there. *If they're drawing penises on the shower door with my shaving cream again, they can forget about ever seeing the sun again. And if he's making shaving cream boobies on her, I swear I'll make him write I WILL NOT MAKE MY SIS-TER LOOK LIKE PAMELA ANDERSON until his hand falls off.*

When I got to the bathroom, I looked inside and saw something that rocked me to my core.

He was washing her hair.

I stopped, backed up a step, and watched in silence. They didn't know I was there.

He spoke softly to her. He told her it was time to rinse (a step he knows she can't stand) and instructed her to turn her back to the water. He helped her crane her head back to let the water cascade down the back of her head. He positioned his right hand on her back for support and his left hand vertically at her hairline to prevent the spray from going into her eyes.

I felt a tear run down my right cheek. I wanted to explode from the chest. How do they do this? How do they become so special? And how do I forget that they have this incredible capacity to love each other?

Fatherhood plays tricks on you. It sets you up to pound your chest and raise your voice and demand compliance from your children. You learn to presume guilt. And then, without warning, it pulls the rug out from under your anger, leaving you out of breath in a blubbering state of gratitude. I love that about it.

The sight of two caring, special human beings— that I helped to create—displaying kindness and love to one another (without being asked) shattered the mold of what I thought I was, what I thought a Man was. Just as the case was with the onset of my depression a few years earlier, the feeling I had at that moment was unlike anything I'd encountered before. And just like depression, that vision rocked me to the core and forced me to take stock of what was happening around me. The one obvious difference between these two moments was that the former left me awash in numbness and confusion. The latter flooded me with a sense that perhaps my life was just beginning, and that maybe if I did right by my children I would be privy to that sense of life many times over. I felt affirmation. I felt privilege. I felt like a survivor.

How do you know when you're better? How do you know when your depression has abated to the point that you can feel normal again? I'm afraid there's no easy answer for that one. There are times when I feel like this disease will be with me, in varying degrees, for the rest of my days. I still take an antidepressant pill every morning, and no matter how often I wish I didn't have to depend on chemicals to make me feel human, I'm reminded on the days when I skip my meds that the distance between contentment and depression is quite short. But I know now what I need to do to keep myself from crossing that boundary.

The best we can do is learn from ourselves, from our experiences, from our own despair. I learned what I need to do (and not do) to keep myself sane. I learned how to identify the emotional and behavioral triggers and red flags that tell me I need to act in my own defense. I learned that the desire to feel better isn't enough to get better; it requires action and commitment.

But in the end, I suppose the most important thing I learned is that sometimes it takes going crazy for a man to truly understand what it means to be sane.

EPILOGUE

The Little League baseball season was in full swing again this spring, and for the first time since my son began playing, I was not his head coach. I helped out where I could—reminding the boys to keep their heads down when they swing, to use two hands when fielding a grounder, and to stop punching themselves in the nuts to see if their protective cups are still working—but other responsibilities made the time commitment required to act as head coach of the A+ division Red Sox impossible.

But the opportunity to take a step backward, however small, gave me a new perspective—and I liked it. A lot. I credit that to the fact that I could now focus more regularly on a certain little stud who wore number seven, batted left-handed, and looked like a much younger and shorter version of me. As a parent and coach, I have tried to portray myself as an entirely objective observer, but I was beginning to see the preposterousness of that line of bullshit. I *did* live vicariously through my son. I absolutely did. I couldn't see myself becoming one of those overzealous Little League dads who barks at his kid when he swings at a bad pitch, but I was certainly my son's biggest fan. And because I have disavowed my objectivity, I don't mind telling you that my son, number seven, is a very good player.

I was late to Noah's game one afternoon because traffic sucked and it took me a moment to quell the homicidal thoughts I was having about a certain Republican president whose name rhymes with Gorge Tush. I arrived in the second inning, ambled up next to Trevor—an assistant coach and good friend—and asked him how the team was performing.

"Most of them are playing like shit," he said, "but I'm having a really good time watching your son play catcher."

"Is he all over the place?" I asked, assuming Trevor was making a joke.

"No, Danny," he said. "Look at him! He's making plays back there. He's not afraid of the ball like most of the other kids on this team."

Trevor is the rare sort of guy who never learned how to sugarcoat anything. He never camouflages anything with bullshit and never pretends to know something he doesn't. I therefore knew his comments about Noah were genuine. And after a long, soul-crushing day in the office, his analysis of my son washed over me like butter on a hot biscuit. I felt my shoulders relax and the tension leave my body. I felt myself exhale.

I spent the rest of the game watching my son and feeling emotional. It wasn't because I was living vicariously through him as he hit screaming line drives and played the game with reckless abandon. It wasn't because I thought his strong play was somehow a reflection on me or the efficacy of my coaching, my fathering, and my own passion for the game. It was because he was having fun. It's as pure as anything I've ever seen: a seven-year-old boy playing baseball, getting dirty, sliding when there's no need to do so just because it's fun to get dirty. He had a bright blue Gatorade mustache. He was wearing a heavily weathered helmet that dwarfed his head. And the smile almost never left his face.

When you watch a lot of youth sports, you begin to notice the attitudes and postures of the kids. Some hate it and look miserable. Some play because they want to make their parents happy. Some try their hardest and strike out every time, but they persevere because once they've felt the rush of hitting a ball on the sweet spot of the bat, they can't wait to feel that euphoria again.

It's the same as what we experience as adults. Some of us are miserable and depressed. Some of us do what we must because we feel obligated or stuck; it's our job to keep going. Some of us are pure blue collar, clocking in and out every day because it's all we know. And like the boys, we persevere because we have faith or hope that we eventually will begin or continue to *feel* something.

I wonder sometimes if the experience at the baseball field that day would have been possible if I hadn't swallowed my light yellow capsule-shaped antidepressant pill that morning after I brushed my teeth. I wonder if I would even have noticed the unmitigated joy on my son's face. I wonder, if the hours of therapy had never happened and the deluge of tears had never been cried out, would I even have had the strength to get out of bed that day? I'll never know the answer to that but I do know this: I'm stronger than I thought. I'm strong enough to feel compassion for my father and support him while he finally examines his own childhood. I'm strong enough to be the responsible, reliable father my kids deserve and the loving, supportive husband my wife intended to marry. And that, for now, is strong enough.

In the end, getting back to being me took far more than waiting for myself to feel better or drowning myself under a wave of beer or shielding myself from the outside world. It meant letting go of the instinct for self-protection so I could open up about who I am, who I thought I was, and what I believed. It meant learning how to live again.

ACKNOWLEDGMENTS

Writing this book was as much a reminder of my good fortune as it was an excavation of my past. I'm more excited about this section of the book than any other because it gives me the opportunity to put into writing how much I value the friends (old and new) and family who played such an enormous role in the achievement of this goal.

This book was Karen Gerwin's idea, and if that's not going above and beyond the typical "literary agent" job description, nothing is. Thank you, KG, for enduring my incessant "Why isn't anything happening?" calls, for responding to my constant need for validation, and for quite literally changing my life with your support, encouragement, and advocacy. I'm extraordinarily grateful to everyone at The Creative Culture, and to Karen's husband, Michael Stoopack, who involuntarily became a good friend (in spite of the fact that he's a Yankee fan).

There is no thank-you effusive enough for Kara Cesare, my editor at NAL. I nearly leapt out of my skin when I learned we'd be working together, and you have validated that enthusiasm with a level of editorial guidance and evenhandedness I always hoped I would find. Thanks for taking a chance on my "humorous depression memoir" and for confirming that I am exactly two degrees of separation from Kevin Bacon (which, given his last name, is probably the minimum allowable distance for a Jew). Thanks also to Kara Welsh, Lindsay Nouis, Philip Pascuzzo, Tom Haushalter, and everyone at NAL.

I owe an enormous debt of gratitude to Jen Lancaster, who went above and beyond the boundaries of friendship to make sure this book got published. Thank you, Martha Kimes, Rebecca Woolf, and Stefanie Wilder-Taylor for holding my hand, kicking my ass, and writing books after which I modeled my own. I flatly would not have been able to write this book without your selflessness and support. Thanks also to Alice Bradley, Eden Kennedy, Mike Adamick, Rachel Shukert, Leah Peterson, Rachel Mosteler, Sean Slinksy, Jen Mathews Friedman, Jason Avant, Angella Dykstra, and Kyran Pittman.

The readers of DadGoneMad.com have given me more than five years of unfathomable love, support, and validation. You made me believe I could write, and that what I had to say might be at once valuable *and* entertaining. I can't begin to articulate how much your encouragement and allegiance mean to me. Thanks, all of you.

Special thanks to David (Rappin' Davey W from Alonim) and Heather (H-Dawg) Wittenberg, the Raab family, Karen Raab, Mickey and Rita Chemers, the Bowers family, Marty (the Cheese Whisperer) and Julie Florman, Downtown Gary Brown, Pam Honsberger, Brian Gurwitz, everyone I know whose last name is Braun, Rowen, Gillman, Wasserman, Kaufman, Cohen, Griffin, Lezak, Wittenberg, or Louis, the entire TBS community, and my boys (young and old) from South Sunrise.

Susan Shalit, your positive impact on my life cannot be overstated. I'm still extraordinarily pissed off that you moved away, but I will suspend my bitterness long enough to say thank you for helping me save myself. Okay, now I'm pissed again.

My big sister, Deb, makes me happy to be alive. Thanks for being there to hold my hand through the hard times and for being here to celebrate the good times. Even though you threw a frozen, stale bagel at my eye when we were teenagers (*on purpose!*), I love you like a fat man loves cake. (You too, Benj, Max, and Annie.)

Mom and Dad, your unremitting support of this book—and *me*—is extremely important. You'll never know how much I treasure your selflessness and enduring love. Thanks for always supporting my writing, even when I write about dirty sex, swear like a drunken sailor, and expose troubling memories. Also? That thing about smoking pot out of a Mountain Dew can? Deb made me do it.

Noah and Julia, you are my favorite people in the world. I love you with all my heart, all my soul, and all my strength. You make me proud just by being yourselves and I can't imagine my life without you. Now that I'm finished writing this book, we can go to Starbucks together any morning you want.

Sharon, your love is the best antidepressant I can fathom. Your beauty, inside and out, was the single greatest factor in my recovery from depression and in my ability to put that harrowing experience into words. You believed in me even when I didn't. You hung in there with me when mortal beings might not have. Your support and faith in me, warts and all, reaffirm my belief that I'm the luckiest man around. I could fill an entire book with the reasons why I love you, but primary among those is that you are the most caring, loving, giving human being I've ever known. I love you.

ABOUT THE AUTHOR

Danny Evans authors the popular, award-winning blog DadGoneMad.com. His writing has appeared in *Good Housekeeping, Southwest Airlines Spirit, Orange Coast,* and other national and regional publications. Danny lives in Southern California with his wife, Sharon, and their two children. This is his first book. Learn more at DannyEvansBooks.com.